SHAME
ERASED

The punishment that brought us peace was upon Him and by His wounds...HEALED.

LEE SHIPP

ISBN (paperback): 979-8-88759-028-8
ISBN (eBook): 979-8-88759-029-5

Table of Contents

INTRODUCTION

HE TOUCHED ME

S hame is an unpleasant, self-conscious emotion often associated
with negative self-evaluation; motivation to quit; and feelings
of pain, exposure, distrust, powerlessness, and worthlessness
(From Wikipedia, the free encyclopedia).

Shame is the human condition. It is the corruption working in
us. To be cured of shame is to become somebody new, somebody
different. The Gospel of Jesus offers this to all. One touch from Jesus
can cause you to become a new creation; shame is erased.

The Law of God exposes our shame; as well, it shines a light on
our guilt. Therefore, we cannot hide. The reason we feel shame is due
to the fact that God has left us no dark place to hide. As the Lord
called Adam from behind the trees of the garden, so the Lord has
called all of us from our hiding places. He wants us to walk out in
the open to meet Him. He wants us to come with the full extent of
our shame. He is not waiting for us to come so He can humiliate us;
instead, He wants us to come so He can cover us, heal us, and save
us from our shame. He can erase it!

THE SYMPTOMS OF SHAME

Check yourself. Go ahead, give yourself a quick self-evaluation.
Do you need this book? Here are the symptoms of shame.

You feel humiliated.
You want to hide.
You want to die.
You want to be left alone.
You want to be someone else.
You are embarrassed.
You cannot look people in the eyes.
You cannot let people get close to you.
You are hiding something.
You are sick with no cure.
You are guilty.
You are excessively proud.
You are loud.
You have mastered the art of distraction, lest anyone see who you really are.
You degrade people.
You cut people down.
You expose the faults of others.
You are a hypocrite.
People pity you.
You have no real friends.
People fear you.
People do not know how to treat you.

Don't confuse shame with guilt. And don't fall for the lie that a few more good deeds will erase your guilt and shame. The internet publishing site *Very Well Mind*, defined the difference between shame and guilt as two distinct things. "Shame refers to something about your character or who you are as a person that you believe is unacceptable." Guilt, on the other hand, "is ... something that you have done. It refers to something you did wrong or a behavior that you feel bad about."

Google explains, *"Guilt is a feeling you get when you did something wrong, or perceived you did something wrong. Shame is a feeling that your whole self is wrong, and it may not be related to a specific behavior or event."* (Feb 18, 2021).

CAN THE SHAMED REALLY BE HEALED?

Before we begin, let us once again review the definition of shame. Shame is an unpleasant, self-conscious emotion often associated with negative self-evaluation; motivation to quit; and feelings of pain, exposure, distrust, powerlessness, and worthlessness.

Shame is a negative self-evaluation of ourselves because our conscious is fully aware that we are broken. There is an evil in us. Consider how Jesus will answer the feelings of our infirmity.

First of all, think about the feeling of pain. The Bible revealed Jesus as the healer. He not only healed people of their physical suffering, but many who were tormented and depressed. Secondly, consider that shame is the feeling of exposure. The feeling that everyone can see who and what you really are. Jesus covers the exposed. He gives them a new identity.

Your distrust is another monster Jesus will conquer. People do not trust you. You do not trust yourself. But Jesus knows everything about you. Nothing in you or about you surprises Him. Jesus does not hope you will make something wonderful out of yourself. Rather, Jesus is excited about what He will make of you through His grace.

Your worthlessness will be transformed into glory by Jesus. You will be given value and brought into the Lord's family. Though many may continue to disown you on earth, Jesus will never be ashamed to claim you as His very own.

THE GRACE TO HOPE AGAIN

In this book you will discover the reality of hope that is in the gospel of Jesus. You will be invited to let Jesus in ... to let Jesus touch you. You will find that He alone has the ability to erase your shame and to heal you by making you a new person. This is not "pie-in-the-sky" fantasies. This is the fact, and millions upon millions of people through the centuries have all joyfully proclaimed this healing touch of Jesus.

I speak of touch because many who are shamed are scared to be touched. For many reasons the shamed like to keep people at a distance. However, you must let Jesus get close enough to touch you. You must want His touch.

Furthermore, there are many who will read this book who have trusted in Jesus but continue to deal with shame. Many who believe in Jesus are shocked to find themselves behaving the way they do. They are ashamed to consider their awful sins against God. It is very possible that the people in our churches are suffering from the greatest blows of shame. They wonder, "It's one thing for God to pity the lost, but how could God pity me? Am I unsavable? Is God through with me? How could Jesus possibly want anything to do with me?"

You will discover that this book is not simply for the lost hiding behind trees and living in the darkness. This book is for those hiding in the church behind hymnals and pews. This book is for churchgoers as well as those who "would never darken the doors of a church." This book is for believers who have realized that they are still falling short of God's desires for them. This book is also for those who secretly want the hope that is in Jesus, but have never trusted in Him before. This book is the loud declaration of hope for those who wonder if God still loves them. The answer is, yes! Jesus is not only the sinner's Savior, but He is also the saints High Priest who saves to the uttermost those who come to God by Him (Hebrews 7:25).

Chapter 1
THE CURE FOR SHAME

Shame is born out of sin. From the abscesses of darkest fears and horrid guilt, shame is spawned, germinating within you such devastation and embarrassment as to cause you to flee to utter gloom and isolation. Shame will drive you to hide behind trees, religion, good works, or beneath the dark veils of addictions and sadistic narcissism. Shame is spawned from sin. Shame is the inner misery that we are cruelly broken beyond repair. To be honest, you do not even believe you are worth the effort of repair.

It is shame that causes you to hide from God. The feeling of absolute humiliation and dishonor convinces you that the only fitting thing for people so worthless and disgusting is God's destructive wrath. You are worthless, hated, despised; there is no place for you— "Just leave me to my darkness."

Shame is deep. It is not just something that happens to you. It is something within you. People only treat you the way they do because shame is what you are. Inferior. Weak. Rejected. Alienated. Powerless. Inadequate. Embarrassed. Defeated. Humiliated. Different. Ignored. Ridiculed. Insulted. Unclean. Defiled. Disgraced. Dishonored. Outcast. Worthless. Filthy. Unlovable. Loathed. Shunned. Discarded. Scorned. Disgusting. Repulsive. Vile.

You try. But everywhere you go and everything you do always ends up the same. Something is wrong with you. You are dirty. Even worse, you are contaminated. There is a difference between being a bit muddy and harboring a deadly contagious virus. Someone can wash off the mud, but to be touched by shame makes recovery seemingly impossible. So, you try other ways. You cut yourself. If you could just bleed, then maybe the disgusting monster would be let out. But this doesn't work either; you just bleed and become more shamed.

If you were a different person, then others would love you. But it's too late; you were born! The best you can hope for is to live unnoticed and, hopefully, death will come as a gracious relief. You live shunned. People avoid you; they reject you; they ignored you. Why? Because you are a disgrace. You are less than human. When you walk into a room, backs are turned. You get the sense that your presence just ruined everybody's party. They ignore you. It is as if you were naked, but you can't help it. After all, you tried to hide.

People begin to look your way … giggle … whisper. You know they are having fun at your expense; you feel you belong in a circus, not life. You are worthless, and it's no secret.

You are of little or no value to those whose opinions matter to you. Why, your very own mother seeks your ruin, wondering how she could have sired something like … you. You are forsaken. You are sure there is something very wrong with you. You are worthless.

THERE IS A CURE

So there you have it, and that is why prisoners of shame live in hiding. There is the thought people are better off without you. You are contagious. No one will ever help you. No one will come to your rescue. Your own family just wants your existence to have been a bad dream.

But you are not a bad dream. You are a person, hurting and broken. You are hoping for someone to help you, to cure you.

What hope is there? Hope is Jesus. The only One who loves you the way you are and is powerful enough to transform your shame into glory! Shame can be erased. Though shame is powerful; it is not almighty—God is! Only God can break its power.

God doesn't ignore your dilemma. He knows its origin stems from your rebellion against Him. He was even wounded by the severity of your shame. God is not trying to convince you that He can love you in your shame; rather, He desires to deliver you from shame and make a new creation to share in His glory. God wants to lift you from the slums of hellish disgrace to the heights of honor—to be made His very own child!

It is your indwelling sin that causes your shame; therefore, Jesus bore your sin and shame that you may be free and become the bearer of His very own holiness and glory. In place of your shame, God wants to give you Jesus! Christ in you is the hope of glory (Colossians 1).

THE GOSPEL IS THE CURE

Possibly, one of the most crucial scriptures in the Bible is often the most neglected. Actually, I cannot remember hearing a preacher using it as a text or subject in all of my Christian life. Even as a minister of over thirty-five years, I have yet to hear other ministers come to this glorious passage. Why? We should run to this scripture constantly and shout it from the housetops. It is the declaration of the gospel. Here it is, "For I will be merciful to their unrighteousness, and their sins and their iniquities will I remember no more" (Hebrews 8:12). What else would you want to hear, shameful sinner? Oh, let us shout for joy and run to this God!

But, how the devil would desire to destroy you … destroy your faith by hiding this truth from you. He would seek to assure you that you are undeserving, disqualified for fellowship with such a holy God as the Lord. Satan would have you believe that God is upset with you and done with you. What's more, your shame agrees with Satan, convincing you that you are but a hideous monster of disgust. But God continues to shout (sadly, there are not enough "gospel" preachers declaring this for God), "I will be merciful to their unrighteousness." Wow! That is why Jesus could say that the Spirit of the Lord was upon Him, because God had anointed him to preach the gospel to the spiritually bankrupt; He sent Him to heal those who had been crushed to pieces (broken to shivers), to preach deliverance to those held in captivity by sin, shame, and Satan, and recover the sight of the blind, to set at liberty those who had been abused (beaten, cruelly and maliciously treated), and to preach to all that this was the year God is accepting you (Luke 4).

Do you hear that? All of you suffering from rejection and shame, all who feel your life is worse than worthless, all who feel that if you disappeared no one would even know you were gone, God is reaching out to you, to heal you, to accept you, to deliver you!

GOD WELCOMES THE SHAMED

God is holy. This holy God bids the unholy and shameful to come to Him. The shamed are welcomed, but God must do something before you can enter His presence. He must make you holy!

He does it. Not by your shedding of blood, but by the blood He shed. Jesus' blood is stronger than your shame. Sin touched you and made you shameful. Likewise, the Holy Jesus will touch you and make you beautiful. There is absolutely nothing you can do to detach yourself from your shame other than believe upon the Lord. There is only one specific remedy that can bring change and transform your shame to glory. Sin touched you, and you became shame. Therefore, righteousness can touch you, and you can become glorious.

You were imprisoned by ugly demonic powers. You can be rescued by the High and Lofty One. You have lived your life under the identity of a rebellious race of sinful, shameful people. Your parents were the first to become a shameful race; you are merely their descendant. God offers you a new identity through the life of another, His Son Jesus!

Through the prophet Isaiah, God cried out to all—to you. Awake, put on strength (Isaiah 52). Are you not tired of this weakness in succumbing to such base feelings and emotions? Awake, put on beautiful garments. You don't have to be naked anymore. You don't have to be ugly anymore. Shake the dust from yourself. You sold yourself for nothing. God will redeem you without money! In your slavery, your abusive masters made you howl and curse God daily. But Jesus has come to redeem you.

Jesus came bringing good news, "How beautiful upon the mountains are the feet of him that bringeth good tidings, that publisheth peace; that bringeth good tidings of good, that publisheth salvation; that saith … Thy God reigneth" (Isaiah 52:7)!

Oh shamed one, break forth into joy! Sing together all of you who wasted your life. Forsake this prison of shame and sin. Depart from it. Don't touch it. Go out of this prison and be clean. For the Lord has laid on Jesus the iniquity of us all.

He was despised and rejected. He was a man of sorrows. He lived with grief. His family and friends hid their faces from Him. Jesus knows shame. He knows abuse. He knows rejection and hate. However, He did it all for you so that you could be free. Jesus is the payment for your redemption from shame. He bore your griefs and carried your sorrows. He was wounded for your transgressions (shame). The correction of your wrongs was meted out upon Him. He was whipped and abused that you might be healed. The Lord has laid on His Son all your shame and iniquity! Why did God do all of this to His Son? He did it in order that He might have mercy upon your unrighteousness!

THERE IS ONLY ONE CURE FOR SHAME

Beloved, when everyone was turning their backs on you, Jesus was giving His back for you. So, what will you do? Will you turn your back on Him, or will you bear His shame as He has borne yours? Most of those who touched you in life were abusive and selfish. Jesus wants to touch you with dignity and honor. Will you let Him?

There is a cure for your shame—only one cure. You must let Jesus touch you and you must touch Him. Make a willful decision to turn away from all the powers that once defined you. Stop allowing the abusive hands to continue molding your life of shame. You now let Jesus mold you into dignity and honor. You declare, "No longer will I give men the power to define who I am or who I shall be. From now on, Jesus will define me. I trust Him!"

Shameful people touched you, but it is time to allow Jesus to touch you. Jesus has a reputation for delivering the shameful people He has touched. Their labels have changed! Shamed people are labeled. They are imprisoned into categories of which there seems to be no escape: Jimmy the backslider, Nikki, the girl who is transgender, Bill the adulterer, Robert the pedophile, June who murdered her husband, Becky who was raped. Jesus sought them out. He was their friend; He was happy to touch them. And when He touched them, He delivered them!

A leper cried to Jesus, "If you will, you can heal me." That's all we know of this man. We don't need to know his name; he is too shameful to have a name. He is just a leper! He lived by a label. But Jesus touched him and healed him (Matthew 8) and he was let back into society. Sinners had everyone gossiping; people love to gossip about the shamed. But Jesus loved to save them. Jesus sought them out, and they sought him out. He was their friend.

Shame makes people feel untouchable. Have you noticed that shame fades when someone else touches you intentionally, in love? Even a woman who suffered abuse and molestation growing up is greatly helped by the sincere love of a husband. But unlike the sincere love of another, Jesus doesn't just help you cope with shame; He erases it!

HOW CAN YOU GET JESUS TO TOUCH YOU?

If Jesus is to touch you, you must touch Him. How do you touch Jesus? He is touched with the feelings of your infirmities (Hebrews 4). He is not touched by how strong you are; rather, He is touched by your weakness. He is not touched by your morality; rather, He is touched by your immorality. He is not touched by your righteousness; rather, He is touched by your unrighteousness: "For I will be merciful to their unrighteousness …" (Hebrews 8:12).

It is the humble and needy, the poor in spirit, who attract the touch of Jesus! "And the whole multitude sought to touch Him: for there went virtue out of him, and healed them all. And He lifted up His eyes on his disciples, and said, Blessed be ye poor: for yours is the kingdom of God" (Luke 6:19–20).

Don't be distracted by the crowds pressing in on Jesus. Keep an eye out for the intentional touch he invites and extends to those He came to seek and to save: the lost, the lame, the blind, the leprous, the discarded, and the sinful.

A woman sick with twelve years of bleeding had to daily cry out to people, "Unclean!" Talk about shameful. She is known as the woman with an issue of blood. She was unclean and untouchable. However, she pressed herself through the crowd, and from behind she touched the border of His garment, and immediately her issue of blood dried up (Luke 8)!

She no longer lived crying, "Unclean." She was no longer known as the woman with the issue of blood; now she is known as the woman who touched Jesus—who Jesus touched!

Crowds were pressing upon Him, bumping into Him. But power went out of Him into her. Why? Because she touched Him with her infirmity!

Are you willing to touch the King? Are you willing to contaminate Him with your shame? Are you desperate enough to ignore the obstacles that stand between you and Jesus? He invites you to come.

When you and Jesus touch, He is not contaminated by your shame; rather, He erases it and confers upon you holiness.

If the gospel of Jesus does not make you stand amazed at the free salvation of forgiveness and grace to those who let Jesus touch them, and instead you believe you must contribute your own works, then you are still a Pharisee trying to work your way out of sin and condemnation to no avail. When you turn toward the holy, your attention is directed to God, the Holy One. He is holy and anything He declares uniquely His is also holy. He has declared us holy—we are saints!

Jesus is the sinner's friend. He is your High Priest. He will not forsake you! He did not forsake you on earth, and He will not forsake you in heaven! Paul said he had a hope in heaven (Colossians 1:5). Hope means expectation. Therefore, what is this hope of Paul waiting there in heaven for him? He reveals this hope in Colossians 1:21–22, "[you] … hath He reconciled in the body of His flesh through death, to present you holy and unblameable and unreproveable in His sight."

In heaven, Jesus will stand beside you and exhibit you as a work of His grace before His Father! Jesus will exhibit you as holy and unblameable and unreproveable in His sight! There is no doubt as to the conflict you live in here. You know your lack or failure in being holy as God is holy. You are full of blame. There are so many things about you that are worthy of being reproved. But in heaven, Jesus shall be with you and demonstrate His perfect holiness and righteousness through your life. There, you will not be an object of shame; rather, you shall be a trophy of His grace!

Chapter 2

JESUS IS NOT ASHAMED OF YOU

Forsaken! The horror of such a feeling. Just ask the abandoned wife, the orphaned child, the grieving friend. There is no feeling like being forsaken. You feel less than human. You feel diseased. You feel ugly. Infectious. Disgusting. Full of shame.

Why do you feel this way? It's because you were forsaken. Someone who was supposed to stay didn't! Someone who wanted you to trust them walked out of your life. Why? It's obvious to you—you were not worth it. You were counting on them. They were supposed to be there. Nothing was ever to tear you apart. That individual was needed. Now, abusive questions bombard the mind: "How will you go on? What will you do? How can you do this alone? How can you ever trust again?" These are fair questions, and experience tells you that it is hard to trust anyone.

But is there someone you can count on? Is there a friend who will remain? A friend who knows you better than you know yourself and will still love you? One who can see into the future and assure you that he/she will never leave? Is there a friend that will stick closer than a brother to you?

I know one! He is true. He is loyal. He knows the future. In fact, He knows every way you will fail. He knows every way you will mistreat and betray Him, but He will not forsake you. He knows the situations that will come, causing you to be ashamed of Him; however, He will not be ashamed of you! He will not forsake you. Even if your father and mother forsake you, He will take you in (Psalms 27:10). He promised you that He would be with you to the ends of the world. His great Apostle declared, "… nothing shall be able to separate us from the love of God which is in Christ Jesus our Lord" (Paul, Romans 8).

The great British preacher, Charles Spurgeon, also commented about the steadfastness of Jesus:

> He will not be satisfied to sit on His throne until you are there. He owned us and His great joy is to share everything with us. He made no protest on the cross—that He might be joined to us—He will not be satisfied till we are enthroned and joined with Him in glory! He would not sit upon His own throne until He had SECURED a place upon it for all who would believe in Him.

> Crown the Head and the whole body shares the honor. Christ's throne, crown, scepter, palace, treasures, robes, heritage, are yours! CHRIST DEEMS HIS HAPPINESS COMPLETED BY HIS PEOPLE SHARING IT: The glory which Thou gavest me have I given them.

> The smiles of His Father are all the sweeter to Him, because His people share them. The honors of His Kingdom are more pleasing because His people appear with Him in glory! More valuable to Him are His conquests, since they have delivered and saved His people. He delights in His throne, because you are there around it! He rejoices in His royal robes, because they spread over you. He delights more in His joy, because you have entered into it!

WHAT DOES IT MEAN THAT HE WILL NOT FORSAKE YOU?

To forsake means to relinquish responsibility—to fail someone who was trusting you, or to refuse to continue with the commitment previously made. When Jesus tells you that He will not forsake you, He is assuring you that He is not like anyone else. All men fail and forsake, even mothers and fathers. But Jesus is assuring you that He is different. He will not abandon you. It is this faith in Jesus that overcomes life. Everything both now and beyond this life depends on the reliability of Jesus. All present and future victories rest upon this surety: from the manger to the cross to the heavens—He has not forsaken you!

HE DID NOT FORSAKE YOU ON EARTH

When our father (Adam) fell in the garden, God did not fail you. He came into that rebellion assuring you that He would rescue you. When Israel failed God in the wilderness by murmuring and rebelling against Him, He did not fail you. When the Israelites spent the entire day dancing before their golden idol, offending and mocking the very God who just delivered them from servitude and abuse, He did not fail you. The morning after, there was manna on the ground (Selah). God's faithfulness to you does not depend on your merit but on His lovingkindness.

When the prophets were rejected and slain, He did not fail you. When the world was in darkness and hope was lost, He did not fail you. A Great Light appeared; the Son of God stepped into our suffering.

He didn't forsake you when you burst into Simon's home to wash His feet. He was not ashamed of you there. He let you touch Him, and He identified Himself with you [When referring to washing His feet, I am referring to the woman in the gospels. She is humanity. As He treated her, so he has treated you]. By going to the cross, He proved that He would not abandon or forsake you. He did not fail you at the cross. He opened not His mouth so that He could give you a victory unshaken and sure.

His payment was so extensive Paul could say, "… things present, nor things to come can ever separate us from the Love of God which is in Christ Jesus." My sin, oh this glorious thought, my sin not in part but the whole, is nailed to the cross and I bear it no more; praise the Lord, oh my soul. He didn't just pay enough…He paid excessively! He didn't just pay a portion, He paid it in full!

He will not forsake you in tribulation or distress or persecution or famine or sword or peril. Not in death or in life. No power in heaven, hell, or earth—nothing that exists or could exist, no height nor depth—no creature can separate me from His love!

He did not and will not relinquish His responsibility for you. He will not refuse to fulfill His commitment to you. He will not embarrass your trust in Him. "Faithful is He that calleth you, who also will do it" (1 Thessalonians 5:24).

You deserve to be forsaken. But He is not a forsaker! His faithfulness is who He is—He is faithful, even when you are not! He does not come to save you because you ARE like Him. He comes to save you that you may BE like Him!

When you are overwhelmed and overthrown and overboard, you are not forsaken. When it is dark, you are not forsaken. When it is hard, you are not forsaken. When the storm is raging, you are not forsaken. He didn't forsake you when you were reprobate, for it was while you were a sinner. And when you had played the prodigal, He did not forsake you. He always had a place for you at His throne of grace. *Oh, what love…no greater love…Grace how can it be, that in my sin—yes even then, You shed Your blood for me.*

He did not forsake you as a sinner; He will not forsake you as a saint! While you were His enemy, while you were the murderer, while you were not good or worthy of salvation to the full extent of what sinners are—that is when Jesus died for you!

While you were a sinner, it was then He expressed His love for you. It was then that He offered you hope. It was then that He defeated your death. It was then that He paid for your crimes. It was then that He destroyed your master, Satan. It was then that He loved you.

If He loved you then, how much more does He love you now? If He loved you in death, how much more does He love you in life? If He would go to the cross for you then, He will go to the Father for you now! If He would not abandon you in that sinful state, He would never abandon you now! If sin could not prevent His love then, can it prevent it now? If your disgusting heart could not cause His love to turn away then, could it now? If, as His very own enemy and murderer, He would desire to buy you to be His own, then consider how much He would want you now!

If when you were a gross sinner, He died for you, is there a gross saint today He would not rescue and save? If when you hated Him He loved you, now when you love Him would He hate you? If when you did not want Him, He laid down His life, now when you need Him, would He forsake you? If He loved you as a sinner, shall He not love you as His child? If He was so good to you as an unbeliever, shall He not be much better to you as a believer?

HE WILL NOT FORSAKE YOU IN HEAVEN

Has the pressure of religion slammed you into the walls of defeat? Have you struggled to achieve holiness only to have a breakdown, and you feel that now all is lost? Forsaken again—now by the religious system.

Are you more focused on discipline and what God requires, rather than on Jesus and the free worship of God? I joyfully exhort you, on behalf of God, "Come by a new and living way!"

The answer is in hearing and believing. Cease from your restless and worthless doings. Repose in full, unquestioning confidence in the one offering of Jesus Christ. Jesus has perfectly satisfied and perfectly glorified God as to the great question of your sin and guilt. It is on this basis that God will never forsake you.

"For by one offering he hath perfected for ever them that are sanctified.

Having therefore, brethren, boldness to enter into the holiest by the blood of Jesus, by a new and living way, which he hath consecrated for us, through the veil, that is to say, his flesh; And *having* an high priest over the house of God; Let us draw near with a true heart in full assurance of faith" (Hebrews 10:12–24).

Jesus prevailed on your behalf. Dare you add to the blood atonement of Christ by some personal work of righteousness? Do you think to earn God's faithfulness? Forget it! He is faithful because you believe in Him; He is not faithful because you are faithful. He is faithful because that is Who He is. Believe what Jesus has done for you.

"We see Jesus...that He, by the grace of God should taste death for every man ... Wherein God, willing more abundantly to show unto the heirs of promise the immutability of his counsel, confirmed it by an oath: That by two immutable things, in which it was impossible for God to lie, we might have a strong consolation, who have fled for refuge to lay hold upon the hope set before us: Which hope we have as an anchor of the soul, both sure and stedfast, and which entereth into that within the veil; Whither the forerunner is for us entered, even Jesus, made an high priest for ever after the order of Melchisedec" (Hebrews 2: 9–11; 6: 17–20).

You can come. Jesus is able to save to the uttermost! He is the mediator of a better covenant. What magnificent wisdom there is in the redemption of God through His Son Jesus. There is power in the blood! In the Old Testament, though God was always merciful and benevolent, the Law demanded justice. In the New Testament, justice is satisfied in Christ! The Law has been nailed to His cross, and for all believers he has perfected obedience! Thank you, Jesus!

Scripture teaches us the believer is accepted in the Beloved—complete in Christ, perfectly forgiven, and perfectly justified through the death and resurrection of Christ; that he can never come into judgment but is passed from death unto life; that he is dead to sin, dead to the world, dead to the law, because Christ has died, and the believer has died in Him.

Christ, by his own blood, entered in once into the holy place. He obtained eternal redemption *for you*. "For if blood of bulls sanctifieth to the purifying of the flesh: How much more the blood of Christ, who through the eternal Spirit offered himself without spot to God, purge your conscience from dead works to serve the living God" (Hebrews 9:11–14).

Jesus is your substituting righteousness before God. Christ is now living and acting at the right hand of God for believers, the children of God, who are passing through this sinful world. He died to make you clean; He lives to keep you clean.

No matter what satanic devices or how many demonic forces are arrayed against you, nothing can ever match the awesome power of God. This God responds to your call for help. He will not forsake you. Sin is defeated.

God now searches for those who are battered and hopeless that He might be strong on their behalf. *God is willing to draw near to those who ask for His help.*

Jesus is your personal High Priest. God the Father obligated Him to this task. "Seeing then that we have a great high priest let us therefore come boldly unto the throne of grace, that we may obtain mercy, and find grace to help in time of need" (Hebrews 4:14–16). He who led your captivity captive was Jehovah Jesus. He who redeemed you was none other than God Himself.

Jesus is your hope in heaven. Paul says, "… the hope which is laid up for you in heaven …" (Colossians 1:5). What is this hope in heaven? It is the assurance that He will "… present you holy and unblamable and unreproveable in his sight" (Colossians 1:22). Jesus will stand beside you and exhibit you as a work of His grace before His Father. He will not forsake you there. He will present you holy, unblamable, and unreproveable before the Father. Jesus does it. There in heaven He owns you and will not forsake you.

Charles Spurgeon beautifully expresses this truth:

> Will the sinners' friend forsake you? No; He will be pleased to own you; He will meet you on the other side of Jordan, and He will say, "Come, my beloved, I have loved thee with an everlasting love, and have bought thee, though thou wast a sinner vile, and now I am not ashamed to confess thee before my holy angels; … come with me, and I will take thee to my Father's face, and will confess thee there."
>
> When the world shall be rolled up like a worn-out vesture, and these arching skies shall have passed away like a forgotten dream; when eternity with its deep sounding waves shall break upon the rocks of time and sweep them

away forever, then, on that sea of glass thou shalt stand with Christ, thy Friend still.

There is no one in heaven talking about how great they are or how worthy they are, but they are all talking about how great and worthy Jesus is. Worthy is the Lamb! He is famous for the sinners He saves, the transgressions He forgives.

Chapter 3
SHAME'S SCAPEGOAT

A ll are guilty. The Bible says there is no one righteous. All have sinned. So, guilt is bearable, because all have it. Shame is different, though all have reasons to feel it. All have experienced shameful things. Some have been devastated by shame. Guilt is the verdict of society based on the fact that you broke its standards. Shame is the stain of what you are or what you have become as a result of what you did or what was done to you. Perhaps you were violated and treated less than human. This mistreatment will stain you and defile you for the rest of your life. Those shameful scars have altered the life you dreamed to live. Perhaps the wretchedness of your lusts finally dominated your actions, and you behaved less than human. You are defiled and a danger to people everywhere. No one wants to be associated with you.

You do not hear a judge say to a defendant, "You are shamed!" Rather, he pronounces, "You are guilty!" Shame is the stain that no jail, detention, or time served can remove. It stays with you far beyond the sentence imposed. It follows you everywhere and catches up to you in the most unlikely places. You cannot escape it, for you wear it. It screams through your eyes, "I am shameful." It shows on your countenance. It is there. Even when others are not aware that you are shameful, the shame in you will find a way to expose itself. It always does.

Shame is associated with dishonor, exposure, nakedness, disgrace, and defilement. The Bible refers more to shame than guilt. Guilt is a legal standing. You are wrong. You have sinned. A person proven guilty expects punishment and needs forgiveness. Shame, however, is so much more brutal than guilt. Shame is the stain on you and the voice within you that screams, "You are despised. You are unwanted." Shame convinces you that you don't belong.

The shamed person expects rejection. You feel worthless and unredeemable. You live in fear that someone is going to expose your stain and devastate your life; therefore, you try hard to hide. Though you try to hide, there is no safe place. Shame is a very real monster that haunts you inside. It is constantly wounding and sealing you off from every hope that you could ever be normal. You hear that monster every time you walk in a room and faces turn away from you or faces turn toward you and people begin to laugh. You are stared at, and you know what they see—they are staring at the stain! You are a monster! You are worthless, and it is no secret.

Shame piles on and other monsters join in. Critical words from the right person add to shame. To pile on shame, all it takes is for the right person to ignore your pain: no action, no response, no words. Nobody defends you—not even those who are supposed to. It is as if you do not exist. The problem is that you do exist, and you wish you didn't. And shame builds. You take on more. You are the reason your parents divorced. It's your fault you were molested. You begin to take the guilt of actions that are not even your fault: the hatred of an unfaithful spouse, the physical abuse of someone who is supposed to love you. It is your fault! What is your fault? That you were born, that you are alive?

CONTAMINATED

Even in the Bible, people were sent outside the camp because they were unclean. They were contaminated and not fit to live in society; they were dangerous to others. Whenever they encountered "normal" people, they had to cry a warning, "unclean" less someone would touch them and become defiled. That's what shame does to people; it announces to all, "I am contaminated!"

If you feel stained with shame, you need to remove that shame. But how? When Jesus was covered with shame, He opened not His mouth. However, many try to remove their shame by blaming others. In an effort to be free from shame, they seek to transfer it to someone else. Adam and Eve's response to shame was to blame one another for what they did.

When you feel relentless condemnation and don't know where to go for forgiveness and cleansing, you look for a way to prove your innocence. People in sin will do one of three things: repent, seek to justify their actions, or point out the sin in others so that their sin is not seen. The tragedy is that no one is cured of shame, but multitudes are left destroyed.

Sadly, I regret that I lived this way for so long—blaming others, justifying myself, refusing to expose myself to God's truth. But Jesus delivered me! I now refuse to serve the monsters of shame. I refuse to destroy other people. Instead, I will "do" truth and come to the light that my sins will be exposed! I will be brutal on my sin and the hideous monster it is (John 3).

Jesus came to save the shamed. He is not afraid to touch you. He is not afraid of being contaminated. He is not afraid of where you live. He is not afraid of your monsters. He is your only hope, and there is not one shamed soul that He will deny! But, dear shamed one, you cannot hide from Him. Please, He is your only hope. You must come to Him. Jesus is your way out of shame! Going to church will not cure you. There are many young men and women who are in churches but don't feel like they belong there. Going to Jesus is the cure!

WE NEED A WAY TO REMOVE SHAME

Listen to this promise: "As far as the east is from the west, so far hath He removed our transgressions from us" (Psalms 103:12). How did God do this? God gave you Jesus! Jesus did not forsake you! What does this mean? It means He opened not his mouth! He did not declare His innocence in order to be accepted. Instead, He remained silent, bore all of your shame, and was completely rejected so that you might be made clean! Listen, if being touched by something or someone shameful can defile you, then touching something Holy can cleanse you. Really think about that. Someone violated you, and you became shamed. Well, if some shameful person can touch you and defile you, then the Holy Jesus can touch you and cure you! "For He hath made Him to be sin for us, who knew no sin; that we might be made the righteousness of God in Him" (2 Corinthians 5:21).

Are you afraid that God will not draw near to you? Oh, banish that fear! It was for you that He came. Jesus said He came for the sick, broken, wounded, defiled, and outcast (Mark 2:17)! His beloved disciple John declared, "And ye know that He was manifested to take away our sins; and in Him is no sin" (1 John 3:5). The Lord has laid on Him the iniquity of us all. Iniquity is the moral evil that is in you. This is the fountainhead of all shame; it is your nature of sin. God announces that He has removed this iniquity and will not remember it again.

In the Old Testament, God provided a temporary provision for Israel's sin and shame. His provision was called a scapegoat, also known as the goat of departure. This goat was to be a picture of Jesus and what He would accomplish with your shame.

The goat was chosen because it represented strong masculinity; it was stout, heavily built, bold, and brave. The goat was impudent: brazenly immodest and unafraid of shame. It was possessed with barefaced audacity and absurdly intruded in an unmannerly way.

Wow! What a picture of Jesus. I just love this. Jesus is the bold and brave one. Of all humanity, it is Jesus who is built with solid strength, unafraid of shame and what others would think of Him. With the boldest audacity, Jesus would intrude into Satan's kingdom of shame and seem absolutely absurd and unmannerly as He begins to rescue the wretched souls who have been held against their will.

The scapegoat was offered once a year on the day of atonement. The offering consisted of two goats; they were for a sin offering. They were presented to the Lord at the door of the tabernacle of the congregation. One would live and one would die.

The one that died was for the Lord, for a sin offering. Its blood was brought within the veil of God's holy place and was sprinkled on the mercy seat. This was done for the transgression of the congregation.

The one that lived was the scapegoat, the goat of departure. This goat was presented alive before the Lord to make atonement, which means to cancel our sin, to cleanse and pardon the sinner. This sacrifice provided mercy and reconciliation with God.

The High Priest would put both hands on the goat's head and confess over it all the iniquities of the congregation (no one is left out). Through this act, the sins were then put upon that goat and the goat, bearing all the iniquities of the congregation, was sent far away. That is a beautiful picture of what God has done for you in Jesus. God can now assure all, "I will be merciful toward their iniquities, and I will remember their sins no more ... I, I am He who blots out your transgressions for my own sake, and I will not remember your sins ... As far as the east is from the west, so far [have I] removed [your] transgressions from [you] ... I will remember their sins and their lawless deeds no more" (Hebrews 8:12; Isaiah 43:25; Psalms 103:12). So let the people rejoice, "He will again have compassion on us; He will tread our iniquities underfoot. You will cast all our sins into the depths of the sea" (Micah 7:19).

All you have to do is touch Jesus! You have to intentionally touch Him. You must touch Him in your shame. It is then that Jesus will touch you back! The gatherings are not enough; the camp meetings are not enough; you must take your needs to Jesus and touch Him.

HOW DO I TOUCH JESUS?

How do you touch Him? As was previously mentioned, He is touched with the feelings of your infirmities (Hebrews 4:15). With your touch, Jesus becomes your scapegoat. With His touch, you become righteous. Touching Jesus is declaring, "I have nothing to offer you ... nothing to contribute. I am worthless and irreparable, rejected ... naked ... contaminated!" That is how you touch Him every time.

It is so sad watching people trying to touch Jesus with their religious self, trying to identify with Him on the basis of holiness. You have no holiness. You cannot identify with Him on that basis. You touch Him with your infirmity—that is what touches Him; that is what He responds to. And trust me, when Jesus touches you back, your stain will be gone! Your shame will be erased. Your monsters will be dead!

As I described in the first chapter, there was a woman in the Bible who was diseased with a bleeding disorder. For years she had to walk among her people crying, "Unclean!" But one day she touched

Jesus—not with her health but with her sickness—Jesus touched her back! She never had to walk unclean again! Now, something else was said about her. People would say, "That is the woman who touched Jesus! That is the woman Jesus healed."

Oh, beloved, will you let Jesus touch you? Are you not tired of all the unsuccessful attempts at trying to remove your stain? Are you not tired of hurting people? Are you not tired of the monsters who haunt you? Shame has been the center of your world for long enough. Shame has identified you far too long. Shame told you how to relate to society and people. Shame was your dreadful companion telling you what was about to happen to you and how people were going to treat you.

Shame is even now trying to tell you that you are too unworthy to be forgiven! But shame is a liar! You are not forgiven because you deserve to be; you are forgiven because Jesus deserves to pardon you. If you want to be forgiven for your own sake, for your own reputation and worthiness, then you will never be forgiven. But if you want to let Jesus have His glory in rescuing your life from such misery, then you shall be forgiven!

TIME FOR A NEW COMPANION

Beloved, it is time for a new companion! It is time for Jesus! He has borne your reproach and shame (Psalms 69). Today you can stand forgiven and holy before God and man because Jesus took the penalty for your sins upon Himself. If you live as though God's forgiveness needs to be helped by your own grief and good works, then you do not understand what He did for you. Grace and faith are the way into God's kingdom. Get used to the kindness of God because you will never understand His mercy! Just get used to being amazed at the gracious King. You will spend all your eternity just saying, "Thank you!"

So, if you want Jesus, you must be willing to accept the honor that goes with the relationship—a royal status ascribed to you, not achieved but given! Oh shamed one, when you enter the kingdom all eyes are on Jesus—not on you or your rights and works. They are fixed on His love, sacrifice, perfection, suffering, and holiness. Look at the scene around the throne of God in Revelation 4–5. No man is singled out or admired. Everyone is singing the same song to the scapegoat!

Beloved, you can be healed. Let Him who touched us touch you. We want you to join our family. We are not ashamed of you! Stop feeling the need for self-protection. Stop with the unbelief! Stop hiding. Stop thinking you will contaminate everything you touch. Come with us to touch the King. Come with us. You will not contaminate us. You do not have to hide. Join us! Join the people of faith and not the self-imposed judges of religion who sneer at us. Don't be one who happens to bump into Jesus in a crowded marketplace. Instead, join those of us who are touching Him intentionally. Come with us. We are going to touch the scapegoat!

Chapter 4
THE GOD WHO COVERS THE SHAMED

The Lord didn't make shameful people. People make shameful people. It is the evil and perverseness in the heart of man that has brought forth the atrocities men have done to one another: the perverse uncle who violates his niece or nephew, the nursery worker betraying the confidence of a parent, the rage of a husband who strikes out at his wife and kids, the unfaithful wife who betrays her husband and her vows. God did not commit these acts of violence—man did! The waves of shame that seek to drown us are the waves we have caused. We threw the stone into the lake that is rocking our boat. God did not do this.

When the Lord made us, we were without shame. "… they were both naked, the man and his wife, and were not ashamed" (Genesis 2:25). However, in just a moment's time the narrative had changed: "… they knew that they were naked … and they heard the voice of the Lord God … and Adam and his wife hid themselves from the presence of the Lord God amongst the trees of the garden" (Genesis 3:7–8).

Why did they hide? Because they realized they were naked. How? What changed for them to know this? "… the eyes of them both were opened …" (Genesis 3:7). Their eyes were opened because they rebelled against God. They chose a life of sin, and shame entered. Here is where shame came into our world. Adam said to the Lord,

"… I heard thy voice in the garden, and I was afraid, because I was naked; and I hid myself" (Genesis 3:10).

There it is, in all of its ugliness. Shame exposed. It is the feeling of being naked, of being exposed, the feeling that everyone can see how ugly you are. Shame is the feeling that you cannot live among people. It is the horrific feeling of believing that everyone can see how diseased you are, how contagious you are. All you want to do is hide.

The shamed just want to be left alone in their cold and depressing world. They just want a place to hide so no one can see them. And why do they hide? Because they are afraid. They are afraid of the judgment and rejection they will suffer. This fear comes from knowing they are guilty. If people saw them the way they see themselves, then they would surely be despised and punished.

HOPE FOR THE SHAMEFUL

What is the hope for the shameful? The persistent God. The God of love. The God who comes into your world and calls for you, "And the Lord God called unto Adam, and said unto him, where art thou?" (Genesis 3:9). The hope for the shamed is the God who will not stop calling you out of hiding until you are confronted with His love. Then you can choose. You can choose to go back into hiding and live in your shame; however, you can choose to be free. You can choose to let God rescue you and allow His love to cover you in the life of another.

That day, in the garden with Adam, was not the only time God has called for you. He did it at the birth of His Son: "… fear not: for, behold, I bring you good tidings of great joy, which shall be to all people. For unto you is born this day … a Saviour, which is Christ the Lord … Glory to God in the highest, and on earth peace, good will toward men" (Luke 2:10–11, 14).

He came in love to save you from your shame. He came to save you from your need to hide. He came to save you from your fear that He will punish you harshly. He came to save you, to heal you, to make you new, and to clothe you with His righteousness. God will get the glory for this feat of redemption, and man will get the mercy. Come on, what else would you want to hear? Forgiven? Ok! Pardoned? Ok! Accepted? Ok. It's all yours!

You cannot escape your shame because it is not what you did or what happened to you; rather, it is what you became. You cannot escape shame because it is who you are. However, you can be saved from your shame because you can be saved from yourself. There is a shame Savior!

BUT YOU TRIED JESUS

I understand what some of you are dealing with. You have tried church. You have tried Jesus; however, it just didn't work for you. You went to church and found it so hard to accept God's love because you had porn on your phone. You tried to worship, but all you could think about was how drunk you were the night before. Your hypocrisy only intensifies your shame, and all you want to do is run and hide. But God will not let you get away so easily. He is calling you to come to Him. Why? Because it gives Him great pleasure to take away your shame. And that is why God sent a band of angels to announce His arrival in a manger. He wanted to let a world shrouded in shame know that He had come to extend "good will" to man, not condemnation.

Good will, wow! Just the thought of that. Good will means kindly intent, delight, pleasure, and satisfaction. It was God's delight and pleasure to free you from your shame and ugliness. It is His disposition to heal you from your abuses, the devastating sexual violations, the despising acts of selfishness. For this baby Jesus, sent to save you, declared, "The Spirit of the Lord is upon me; He has appointed me to preach Good News (that is so lovely) to the poor; he has sent me to heal the brokenhearted and to announce that captives shall be released and the blind shall see, that the downtrodden shall be freed from their oppressors, and that God is ready to give blessings to all who come to him" (TLB).

THE CHURCH'S COMMISSION

To you, Church, this is your commission: to go into all the world and tell the shamed the Good News of Jesus. It is not your job to point your finger at the shamed. Instead, it is your privilege, rather, it is your good pleasure to point the shamed to Jesus!

When the shamed come into the church, it is your privilege to cover their nakedness, to give them hope. Satan would swallow them up with sorrow. You have to rescue them before Satan swallows them. And how do you rescue them? By confirming the love of God to them.

The shamed come to church thinking, "Nobody is going to like me." So, like them, church! The shamed think, "They are going to reject me." So, accept them, church! Oh, that we would fight for one another as Jesus did for us.

Satan is the accuser of the brethren; don't let him work through you. Instead, overcome Satan's oppression in your brothers and sisters. "... they overcame him by the blood of the Lamb, and by the word of their testimony; and they loved not their lives unto death" (Revelation 12:11). Notice they overcame Satan! It does not say the Lord overcame Satan because the Lord had already overcome him on the cross. Now, it is the responsibility of the Church to exercise that victory for one another. By the blood of the Lamb, by the Word of God, and by fearless loving they fought for one another to live despite Satan's constant accusations.

ENOUGH OF THE DESTRUCTION

There is destruction taking place in the Body of Christ, and many do not understand it. Some abuses occur in the Body of Christ that serve the devil's purposes. These destructive abuses are seen in how the religious try to run others' lives. Young men and women have learned how to rebuke and criticize one another "in the name of Jesus" [I say this sarcastically]. Lost souls sent to our churches are never given the chance to lay hold of the wondrous unshackling experience of Jesus' liberty.

The leaders of the movements that have presided over this carnage are not even aware of the destruction, much like the Pharisees in Jesus' day. They are not aware of the thousands of shipwrecked lives their ministries have caused. There appears to be an almost total disregard by the leaders in these groups of the mounting and appalling destruction resulting from this abuse.

There is no cause for a man seeking Christ to be wrecked by abuse in the House of God. No, no justification for it whatsoever. Therefore, the church should shield men and women from Christendom's corruption. The church should give the shamed an environment of liberty, grace, and hope. The church should lead the shamed into the fullness of Christ without fear of destruction and rejection.

The high level of bitterness and isolation among Christians these days only reveals the bankruptcy of love among God's children. Yet all the while, these abusers would proudly proclaim that they are strong in God's love!

No man is more mature in Christ than the man who can love at all times, to all people, under all circumstances! Love is never more manifest than when it is suffering in order to extend forgiveness to those who have caused its sorrow and wounding!

Love cannot forsake! Love cannot run away! It must stay and fight and labor for the benefit of those by whom it is offended. To God, this would be the fruit of believers' lives. If you would submit to the Holy Ghost, He would make you more than scholars; He would make you apostles of Love! And if He could mature you in Christ, bringing you to the point of being a loving people, revival would be ceaseless in the House of God! Love does not run and hide because love cannot live alone. Love would rather be crucified by you than live alone without you. This is what the Holy Ghost is conforming you to. This is the love that causes faith to work!

BELIEVERS OUGHT TO FORGIVE AND COMFORT

Satan must not be given ground in the Church. Believers ought to forgive and comfort those who are seeking Christ lest they are swallowed up with sorrow. You should demonstrate and confirm the love of God to one another—by loving one another in sincerity. Paul said that if you do not extend love and forgiveness, then Satan would get an advantage over YOU (2 Corinthians 2). Satan would not simply swallow up the sorrowful, he would get an advantage over the Church (2 Corinthians 2:11). An unforgiving and harsh spirit will fall prey to Satan's plans.

This is a stern warning to the believers. It is a stern warning for preachers as well. There are two types of preachers/believers in the Church: those who are ministers of the letter and those who are ministers of the Spirit. The letter kills, but the Spirit gives life. It requires a miracle to become a minister of the Spirit. It only requires Bible knowledge to be a minister of the letter. The sad truth is that both groups believe they are right and serving God. However, those of the letter are killing the shamed "in the name of Jesus."

The preachers of the letter are sincere. Preachers of the letter are not preaching error—they are preaching the letter, and the letter is correct. They want their people to thrive and live with power and victory. They really desire the best for others. However, instead of giving them the ability to REIGN IN LIFE, they bring death. They get a Word and with it rebuke the failure of the people. This exploitation of the believer's failure and shame occurs week after week by those who preach the letter. The Church dwindles and the preacher doesn't understand. The preacher of the letter simply reasons, "I'm preaching the truth! But people do not want to hear the truth." But that is not the truth. The shamed do want truth. They want the Truth that brings life! In every service, the shamed are at the altar hoping this time they will be able to perform the demands of the letter. There is not a lack of repentance in these ministries; there is a lack of grace.

Ministers of the Spirit give life. They preach hard. They preach truth. There is conviction. There is grace. The love of God and the hope of God fills the message. They assure people who are in Christ that they are accepted in the beloved. The ministers of the Spirit of life assure the shamed (that come into our churches) that God is excited that they have come.

The shamed are aware that God knows everything about them. Their sins are exposed. Where the ministry of the Spirit of life is at work, the shamed are called out of hiding. Their shame is dealt with. Under the ministry of the Spirit of life they have the keen understanding that God will accept them and sanctify them through the blood of His Son. However, in the churches where there is the ministry of death, the shamed are convinced that God will only accept them if they first become holy. Those of the letter insinuate,

"We will approve of you if …" Those of the Spirit confirm, "We approve of you because …"

Ministers of the letter reinforce the fear and condemnation of the shamed. They speak to the conscience of men and not to their spirits. They show them that they are wrong and that they are sinners, then give them the rules by which they should change their behavior. They affirm that their shame is a disgrace and make the shamed feel they must become different before God will love them. Like Adam, the shamed hide behind prayers, deeds, and religion. They are afraid and grow more hopeless because they are reminded every week by the preachers of the letter of their constant failure. Ministers of the Spirit must defeat this fear.

When the letter was being given on Sinai, amid the quaking mountain, the thunder, and the lightning, the people were afraid of God and rightly so. However, when the Spirit was being given on Calvary, multitudes drew near to God: "And I, if I be lifted up from the earth, will draw all men unto me" (John 12:32).

THE SHAME SAVIOR

The greatest minister of the Spirit, Jesus, delivered people from their shame. He preached to them Good News. He proclaimed to them the acceptance of God. He assured them that He had not come to condemn but to save. The children ran to Him. The sinners flocked to Him. And the woman at the well, who was living with a man after five failed marriages, brought an entire city to Him. Why? He was life! People were safe in His love. Likewise, the New Covenant minister (of the Spirit of life) will not give place to Satan. As Paul testified to the Corinthians, "… I do not have dominion over your faith, but are helpers of your joy: for by faith ye stand…. I would not come again to you in heaviness. For if I make you sorry, who is he then that maketh me glad…. [God] … hath made us able ministers of the New Testament; not of the letter, but of the spirit: for the letter killeth, but the spirit giveth life…. Now the Lord is that Spirit: and where the Spirit of the Lord is, there is liberty" (2 Corinthians 1: 24; 2:1–2; 3:6, 17).

Make up your mind that you are going to forgive and free everyone just as you need to be forgiven and set free. Bear in your body the marks of Christ, which are love.

Others have said this as well: "You have life before you. Once only you can live it. What is the noblest object of desire, the supreme gift to covet? We have been told that the greatest thing in the religious world is faith; however, faith cannot work without love" (Henry Drummond). "The one great need in our Christian life is love, more love to God and to each other. Would that we could all move into that Love chapter and live there" (D.L. Moody). Paul said "the greatest of these is love." Peter declared, "Above all things have fervent love among yourselves." John the beloved Apostle testified, "God is love."

> Take any of the commandments. "Thou shalt have no other gods before me." If a man loves God, you will not require to tell him that. Love is the fulfilling of the law. A man in love with God would never dream of taking God's name in vain. If he loves God, he must love man… for God loves man! It would be preposterous to tell him not to kill. You could only insult him if you suggested that he should not steal —how could he steal from those he loved? He would never covet what his neighbors had. He would rather they possessed it than himself. Christ's one secret of the Christian life, the key to fulfilling all the law—LOVE!
>
> Missionaries can take nothing greater to the heathen world than the LOVE OF GOD working within their own character. What is love in the character? Patience, kindness, generosity, humility, courtesy, unselfishness, good temper, guilelessness, and sincerity.
>
> Take into your sphere of labor, where you also mean to lay down your life, that simple love, and your lifework must succeed. You can take nothing greater; you need take nothing less. You may take every accomplishment; you may be braced for every sacrifice; but if you give your body to be burned, and have not love, it will profit you and the cause of Christ nothing.

We hear much of love to God; Christ spoke much of love to man. We make a great deal of peace with heaven; Christ made much of peace on earth. [Consider] Christ's Life: He spent a great portion of His time simply in making people happy, in doing good turns to people. There is only one thing greater than happiness in the world, and that is holiness; and it is not in our keeping; but what God has put in our power is the happiness of those about us, and that is largely to be secured by our being kind to them.

The greatest thing a man can do for his Heavenly Father is to be kind to some of His other children. I wonder why it is that we are not all kinder than we are? How much the world needs it! How easily it is done! How instantaneously it acts! Love never faileth: love is success, love is happiness, love is life.

Where love is, God is. He that dwelleth in love dwelleth in God. God is love. Therefore love. Without distinction. Without calculation. Without procrastination, love. Lavish it upon the poor, where it is very easy; especially upon the rich, who often need it most. Most of all upon our equals, where it is very difficult, and for whom perhaps we each do least of all. Give pleasure. Lose no chance of giving pleasure; for that is the ceaseless and anonymous triumph of a truly loving spirit.

I shall pass through this world but once. That good thing, therefore, that I can do, or any kindness that I can show to any human being, let me do it now. Let me not defer it or neglect it, for I shall not pass this way again.

Withholding love offends the Holy Ghost and is the proof that we never knew Him nor cared for Him! It means that He suggested nothing in all our thoughts, that He inspired nothing in all our lives, that we were not once near enough to Him to be seized with the spell of His compassion for the world. It means that: I lived for myself, I thought for myself, for myself, and none beside—just as if Jesus had never lived, as if He had never died. (Henry Drummond, The Greatest Thing In The World).

I selected these comments because it seems all too common for people to run away. Your feelings get hurt; a legitimate offence occurs and you are offended. The typical response is to run, flee, and forsake the body. But is this love? Does the love of God run? When your sin offended God, did He run and forsake you?

> Love, just because it is love, exposes itself to all risks—even the risk of being misused by the wicked—in order to win all. We must not give up teaching love for one's enemies, even though, for a time, God haters profit at our expense. We believe that the Word is God and in the end this Word will change the hearts of even those who hate God. (Richard Wurmbrand, page 131, Extreme Devotion).

Chapter 5
MANNA ON THE GROUND

There is something different about the love of God and the love of His children. And there is something altogether different about the love that comes from the religious who claim they are serving God and the love of God. God has always been a refuge to the weak. God has always been a strong tower to those fleeing from their enemies. The one place on earth where hope should reign supreme is the Church of the Living God. But how often do the weak and fleeing find themselves swallowed up with sorrow rather than the refuge of God's unfailing love? And in God's very own church!

Consider the goodness and kindness of the Lord. When Israel sinned by worshipping the golden calf, dancing in shame around the golden idols, God was still true to His nature and love! When they woke up the very next morning, there was manna on the ground. Hallelujah—what grace! This is amazing love, amazing grace to the shameful. Picture the morning: remnants of shattered commandments God wrote with His own finger, mingled with manna!

God has hope for shameful people! Satan wants to swallow you with sorrow, but God wants you to enter into the Holy of Holies! Truly! While Aaron is making the golden calf, God is telling Moses how Aaron is to enter His presence and minister to Him. And again, of all the people the Holy Ghost could have picked to preach on Pentecost, He chose the shameful denier (Peter) to preach a message of denial to the multitudes on the streets of Jerusalem! Christians would have never let Aaron serve as High Priest nor would they have let Peter preach the Pentecost sermon!

I am not advocating sin. "Shall we continue in sin that grace may abound? God forbid" (Romans 6: 1-2)! There is no mandate here for disobedience, nor does it make sin less serious. However, I want you to know that when all seems lost, mercy can shine through judgment, and the rainbow of God's promise tells of everlasting hope!

When every hope is dashed, when every noble dream and every holy ambition written with the finger of God Himself upon your heart is shattered, hope can rise again, and grace can chase away the gloom—there is manna on the ground! He has not left you, nor has He left you comfortless!

God said through the prophet Haggai, "According to the word that I covenanted with you when ye came out of Egypt, so My Spirit remaineth among you: fear ye not" (Hag 2:5). God might well have said to His people of old, "For forty years you grieved my Spirit, and yet I never left you!" The daily manna is the proof of God's faithfulness. The cloud by day never failed…the fire by night never diminished—GOD DID NOT FORSAKE! You may grieve and quench Him, and if you do, He will let you know it because He lovingly chastens all His children, but HE WILL NOT FORSAKE YOU.

DESTROYED WHILE SEEKING CHRIST

There is a destruction going on in the Body of Christ, and many do not understand it. Many come to church FULL OF SHAME and sin. They cannot escape the guilt and weight of shame. They are afraid, but they have nowhere else to go. They are seeking salvation in Christ. This is the place they hope to find Him. The shamed are scattered all over the house: some are singing on the platform, some are sitting in the balcony, some are buried in the altar, some are hidden in the back, some are even in the front; but they all are desperately hoping for the same thing. They are hoping you will not see them, and if you do, that you will not hurt them. They are scared because they know they are messed up. They sit in church and wonder what they are even doing there, thinking they are but a foul smell in the nostrils of God, asking, "Why am I even here? If anybody knew me they would cast me out!"

They are among us; they *are* us! God only has one Son who was perfect—Jesus! But yet, the shameful people come, seeking a refuge, hoping for salvation. They come to church after fulfilling their lusts and desires all week and are sick of their hypocrisy—young people praying in tongues, acting serious about God, viewing porn on their phones, and posting in social media images they hope no one ever sees. Oh, the shame we are trying to hide from or trying to be saved from: the shame of not being a person people can love, the shame of not fitting in, the shame of not being liked by others, the shame of fearing that others are going to hurt you, the shame of being afraid that everyone can see right through you, that you are naked and nobody wants you, that people are embarrassed of you, the shame of fearing that you will be rejected and despised.

Let the church fight by love for one another so that all of us who once were covered in shame would not be ashamed of the shameful, but seek their deliverance through the blood of Jesus. And why do the shamed risk so much in coming to church? They are hoping for freedom, for reality, for somebody to help them. They come with the questioning: Is there mercy for me? Is there any hope for me?

Do you have any idea how hard it is for shameful people to get the courage to go to a house full of holy people? Do you comprehend the fear they have to overcome just to be around you?

The shamed walk into a place and hope they will be accepted. They cry within, "I hope I am liked, wanted, known for who I am, and still wanted." They wonder, "What if I fail? Will the church put me away, be embarrassed of me, disown me?"

According to 2 Corinthians 2, Satan seeks to swallow up the people with sorrow by an unforgiving, harsh, and loveless church. Satan swallows his victims by sorrow—not by a lack of repentance but a lack of hope!

Honestly, it is the church that must show the goodness of the Lord. Paul warned the church, forgive them, comfort them, receive them, confirm love to them lest Satan swallow them with sorrow. But too often the sad reality is that few churches have followed Paul's instructions to comfort, accept, and confirm the love of God to the shamed. Smiles are everywhere, but ice is in the hearts. The shamed are not accepted, not allowed into fellowship; they are not approved! Oh, the chilling horror of such rejection in God's own house, and the shamed turn and cry, "I am never going in there again."

Church, do you know that this is a common experience in the house of God? However, that is not the demeanor and love of the God of the house; it is just the imperfect, distorted love of His children. God declares you are accepted in the Beloved! This means that when one walks into God's house, God approaches them with joy that they have come to Him. Knowing everything about you, He makes you know that He longs for you and wants to accept you. He wants you to know how He longs to approve of you through His Son Jesus. He wants you to know that you are approved in the Beloved Son! Religion says, "We will approve of you if ..." God says, "I approve of you because ..."

PREACHERS ARE KILLING PEOPLE

In 2 Corinthians 3, Paul shows there are those who preach the letter (the law). They kill people with the letter. They are not ministers of the Spirit who give life. These preachers of the letter speak to the conscience of men, reinforcing the fear they are living in. They assure the shamed that they are to be shamed; they are wrong, and they are sinners. Their guilty conscience confirms that this letter of truth is right! So, what do they do? Like Adam, they try to hide behind prayers, deeds, and religion. They are afraid and seek freedom from this fear by appeasing the demands of the law—which they will never do! It is the destruction of the letter!

Totalitarian rulers with convictions boldly serve as God's holy emissaries demolishing multitudes...seeking to rob them of the liberty that abounds through Christ!

Because of these abusive lawyers, more people have left the church of Jesus and are not coming back. These totalitarian rulers have wielded two of the most powerful weapons known to man—the Bible and God, to manipulate men for their advantage!

Multitudes are threatened with the letter by preachers who are not sent by, nor anointed with, the Holy Spirit. I wonder if the leaders who preside over this carnage are even aware of the thousands of shipwrecked lives out there. There appears to be total disregard by the leaders in these groups of the mounting and appalling destruction resulting from their preaching of the letter. There is no cause for a man who is seeking Christ to become wrecked. No! No justification for it whatsoever.

For those preachers of the letter, the problem is not doctrine. They preach the letter, and it is true. The problem is hearts. Their disciples are twice the children of hell!

They are young men and women who have learned how to rebuke and criticize one another. These ministers of the letter appeal to the pride in people's hearts, cultivate a self-righteous arrogance, and water and fertilize their destructive tendencies with misplaced scriptures and religious zeal.

This devastation is extremely costly, for if you lose trust in Christians, you have absolutely nowhere to go. Fear and confusion become the order of the day. Young men and women who should have grown up and grown old serving the Lord are ruined forever—Christians aborted, never given the chance to lay hold of the wondrous liberty found in Jesus' grace! Scattered throughout the country and the world are those aborted lives of bitter and shipwrecked people who just simply hoped to find help in Jesus.

But there is a Spirit-anointed minister who brings life. One Bible story in particular depicts the beauty and advantage men are given by God's grace. The scene is set in the house of a religious man who can only relate to God by the law. In the view of these religious elites, sinners and shameful people are contagious and defiled—they have no place among the holy. But on this particular occasion, He, who is grace and truth, is sitting among these holy men. A woman with a horrible reputation for sin finds her way into the room of holy men and falls at the feet of grace and truth. Appalled by her appearance, the holy men take this as an opportunity to frown upon Jesus, surmising that if He were a prophet, He would know what kind of woman this was and would never allow her to touch Him. But Jesus, being the prophet, discerned their thoughts and spoke to the hypocrisy of these men by assuring the woman her sins were forgiven and she had found grace and favor in God's sight.

I cry to you, beloved, to shield men and women from Christendom's corruption. Give the shamed an environment of liberty, grace, and hope. Lead people into the fullness of Christ without fear of destruction and rejection. Pass on to the next generation an experience of Christ that is higher than anything the last generation has known. Press them beyond our spiritual growth and limits in Christ. Then hope. Hope they will best all of us!

MINISTERS OF CHRIST MUST DEFEAT THE FEAR

Men have typically misunderstood God. Fear is oftentimes the culprit. Because we have sin, we fear a sense of future punishment from the Almighty God. It causes us to misunderstand God's desires for us. We filter all religious thoughts through this lens of our guilt and God's justice. We assume that God's motives are of judgment rather than love. Adam in the garden hid from God because of shame and fear. On Sinai, with thunder, lightning, and earthquakes, Israel refused to hear God and told Moses to go before the Lord. But when God came, when Jesus drew near, God's love was shown forth. Sinners were drawn to Him. In Him was hope and love and redemption. Jesus brought grace and truth to the earth! He brought the full revelation of God—God is love! He cried to the people, "I did not come to condemn you." And the children ran to Him; the sinners placed their hope in Him.

Fight fear with love! Perfect love casts out all fear! The church needs to be filled with people who are fighting for one another—a people who are not ashamed of the shamed. Satan is the accuser! If you are accusing people, then it is obvious what spirit is working in you. God's people are those fighting Satan for the freedom of others. They are overcoming Satan's brutal attack by the blood of the Lamb and the word of their testimony! The church is the place where the shamed and wrecked can find refuge and salvation from the scourges of the enemy. It is the place where the repentant will find comfort and the confirmation of love. If you are going to be a Christian, you are going to spend your life forgiving people! Resign yourself, beloved, to this truth: You are going to live to free everyone from everything that separates them from God.

Chapter 6
WHO WINS?

Who wins? Everyone is trying to. Everyone wants to. But who really does? Who reigns in life? Do kings? Numerous kings have sat as sovereigns ruling over great kingdoms, but were they really reigning? Did Caesar reign? What of King James? Queen Mary? No. They were miserable! Did Paul reign? Did he win? He said he did. He testified that he had run his race, he had finished his course, he fought a good fight and kept the faith. Did Jesus win? Did He reign? Jesus, well ... God raised Him from the dead. He triumphed over death. He has a name that is above every name and sits as the power in heaven. Oh, and He has an everlasting kingdom and joy and a joyful kingdom and a joyful people. And love, He has a kingdom of love.

So, can you win? Can you reign over life? The declaration of the gospel is an absolute—yes! God promises to bring everyone who believes in His Son into the victory of His Son. He guarantees them to be more than conquerors, "... thanks be unto God who gives us the victory through our Lord Jesus Christ" (Romans 8). John revealed that the victory which overcomes the world is your faith—your belief that Jesus is the Son of God.

If your relationship with God is on the basis of faith, then nothing can separate you from the love of God other than an unbelieving heart. However, numbers of you are convinced your relationship with God is based upon your ability to measure up to God's demands.

You somehow consider that if you are good enough, then God will be disposed to show you kindness and perhaps answer your prayers. You conceive that your sufferings are the results of your failures and an unhappy and unimpressed God is giving you what you have earned—the just wages of your disobedience.

The gospel of grace shatters this theology. In Romans 4, Paul shows that Abraham did not have a relationship with God on the basis of works. Instead, Abraham walked with God and was justified by God through his faith in God. "For what saith the scripture? Abraham believed God, and it was counted unto him for righteousness" (Romans 4:3).

Furthermore, if you relate to God on a system of debt, then how do you know if you have prayed enough? If you have fasted enough? If you have sacrificed enough? The answer is you don't know. You only hope that you paid the expected price God was demanding. In time, you will discover if you were good enough based on whether God answered your prayers or not.

I have heard preachers manipulate the people through this bartered relationship with God, robbing them of grace and the ability to reign in life. Preachers of the letter (2 Corinthians 3) will cry, "If you had fasted just one more day the answer would have come." Or they may say, "The reason we do not have revival is because we have not sacrificed enough; we have not repented enough." This is wrong; it is not grace. Furthermore, you are never sure if you will get anything from God.

When we live by grace through faith, the answer is always certain and the answer is always, "Yes!" Do you ever see Abraham condemning himself because of his failure? Abraham sinned. Do you ever hear Abraham concluding that God was finished with him because he sinned and disobeyed God? No, you don't. Abraham did not live under the law. The Law would not be given for another four hundred years after Abraham was dead. Abraham lived in grace. He, by grace, reigned in life. Beloved, this is the liberty the gospel is calling us into. All the promises of God are in Christ Jesus: Yes, and Amen! Can you believe this? Can you live by the abundance of His grace, or do you demand a relationship with God that is based on debt? Abraham did not live that way; he lived by faith!

If a man is determined to work for his relationship with God, then he cannot live by grace; this is his choice, not God's. Likewise, the man who chooses to not work but rather to believe on Him that justifieth the ungodly, he shall be counted righteous by God (Romans 4:4–5). David referred to this man of faith as blessed and forgiven before God.

A RELATIONSHIP OF FAITH OR DEBT

God did not establish His promises to Abraham on the basis of the Law, but through the righteousness of faith. The Law makes faith void. Likewise, faith makes the Law void. Furthermore, if the promise is made upon law and debt, then the promise is void, for all men have failed, sinned, and fallen short of God's demands (Romans 4:14–16). The only thing that a man living by the Law can expect is God's wrath. But when a man chooses to live by faith, then the Law is made void, and where there is no Law there is no transgression (Romans 4:15).

"Therefore it is of faith, that it might be by grace; to the end the promise might be sure to all the seed; not to that only which is of the law, but to that also which is of the faith of Abraham; who is the father of us all ..." (Romans 4:16). Abraham's confidence was never in himself or that he could fulfill God's demands or that he could produce an heir by some working of his own power. Instead, he lived by faith, "... being fully persuaded that, what he had promised, he was able also to perform" (Romans 4:21).

Just as Abraham had access to God through faith, so do you as well. You do not have to live hoping in yourself. You do not have to live wondering if you have been good enough for God to accept you. Instead, you can enter into God's righteousness by faith and there you can live and love God, "Therefore being justified by faith, we have peace with God through our Lord Jesus Christ: By whom also we have access by faith into this grace wherein we stand, and rejoice in hope of the glory of God" (Romans 5:1–2).

HOW DO WE REIGN?

Now, let us come back to the victory of this life. There are a people who reign in this life! The Bible assures you of a true and tangible victory. Not a hollow confession of wishes, but a true and manifest power. Not a testimony with clenched teeth that says "I am not depressed," but a radiant demeanor of joy and freedom. The once shamed people of the earth are to be clothed in this beauty! How do we reign? "For if by one man's offence death reigned by one; much more they which receive abundance of grace and of the gift of righteousness shall reign in life by one, Jesus Christ" (Romans 5:17). There it is ... the gift of victory. The victorious life is the one that is receiving an abundance of grace and the gift of righteousness.

Instead of receiving this grace, it becomes evident that multitudes continue to struggle to live by their works in an effort to prove their sincerity and worth to God. They constantly feel that if they pray enough, fast enough, give enough, or suffer enough, then God will be in their debt to help them? You will never reign in life that way. Sure, they are saved by grace, but somehow they are trapped into thinking they must continue in works.

If you are not enjoying this power in Jesus, it is because you are being denied an abundance of grace. Perhaps you are sitting under those who are ministers of the letter. Perhaps you are not open to live by grace; you believe that living by grace is not enough to gain the favor of God. Your defeat is the proof of your error!

The hope for all men is the gospel of God's grace! Has the pressure of religion slammed you into the walls of defeat? Have you struggled to achieve holiness only to have a breakdown, and you feel that now all is lost? Are you more focused on discipline and what God requires than on Jesus and the free worship of God? Then I joyfully exhort you, on behalf of God, to come by a new and living way!

The Bible reveals in Colossians that as you received Him, so walk in Him. How did you receive Him? According to Ephesians 2, it was by grace through faith. And that is how you walk and live and win—you live by grace through faith.

Paul explained to the Romans that the consequences of one man's disobedience resulted in the death of all people. These people didn't do anything to suffer the consequences of death and sin but to be born. Adam's sin and judgment was imputed to all of his children. Unless heaven can rescue, humanity is doomed. So, God, by His love and mercies, offered life and righteousness the same way. If one man's disobedience makes many sinners then one man's obedience will make many righteous. This righteousness will be a gift imparted to those who will believe in His Son Jesus.

> For if by one man's offence death reigned by one; much more they which receive abundance of grace and of the gift of righteousness shall reign in life by one, Jesus Christ. Therefore, as by the offence of one judgment came upon all men to condemnation; even so by the righteousness of one the free gift came upon all men unto justification of life. For as by one man's disobedience many were made sinners, so by the obedience of one shall many be made righteous. Moreover, the law entered, that the offence might abound. But where sin abounded, grace did much more abound: That as sin hath reigned unto death, even so might grace reign through righteousness unto eternal life by Jesus Christ our Lord (Romans 5:17–21).

Your victory rests upon two things: the gift of righteousness and receiving an abundance of grace. Notice the victory is given as a gift to those who will receive. It is by faith.

THE GIFT OF RIGHTEOUSNESS

Righteousness is a gift from God; it cannot be earned. The law was never given to make you righteous or help you to be righteous. The law was given to prove your guilt before God. The law was to lead you in desperation to salvation through the grace of the Lord.

As Abraham believed God and it was accounted to him as righteousness; likewise, you are joined with him in righteousness if you also believe God. This righteousness is a gift whereby you stand with God and God with you, as though you had NEVER done one thing wrong!

Now, here is the problem. Many believe salvation is by grace through faith, but keeping the law is the way of sanctification.

The Bible clearly teaches that you are saved by grace through faith (Eph 2) and that you are sanctified by grace through faith. "As ye have therefore received Christ Jesus the Lord, so walk ye in Him" Colossians 2:6. But people do not live there. Instead, many live trying to earn God's favor by dead works. Victory is not promised to someone believing just one of these truths. You cannot live in the victory by simply receiving the gift of righteousness; you must also receive the abundance of grace.

THOSE WHO RECEIVE AN ABUNDANCE OF GRACE

Victory is for those who receive an abundance of grace! Sadly, many will not. It is not because God has refused to offer them grace. Instead, they have spurned His goodness. Multitudes who gather in the name of Jesus each week to worship the Lord are squandering His grace and living lives of defeat and tragedy.

If by the abundance of grace you reign in life, then how can you not want more grace? What person in need of God would ever say, "Enough of the grace; give me something else now!" If by the grace of God "I am what I am," then how can you not desire more grace? If in your weakness His grace is sufficient, then how can you not cry for more grace? If grace is God's direct influence and power exerted upon your heart and life, then how could you say God's grace is not enough to keep you holy and live pleasing in His sight?

Grace is Christ in you as the hope of glory. Grace is God working in you both to will and do of His good pleasure. It is by the indwelling Christ that you reign in life and are able to have everything. All the passages about the indwelling work of the Holy Ghost and His power in the believer are grace working!

EVERYTHING COMES BY THIS GRACE.

Therefore, everything comes to the believer by grace. Everything you need to be holy, to be faithful, to be victorious, to be used, to be happy is by abundant grace. It is not grace and other things. You would not ask a preacher to teach you about grace and also about conviction, as though they were separate from one another. It is not grace and now speak on holiness. It is not grace and now speak on being faithful and not sinning. It is not grace and now speak on discipline. It is not grace and now speak on separation from the world. It is not grace and now speak on repentance.

When you speak on grace —the abundance of God's help—you are speaking on holiness. When you speak on grace, you are speaking on discipline and works of faith. When you speak on grace, you are speaking on being faithful and not sinning. When you speak on grace, you are speaking on repentance. When you speak on grace, you are speaking on conviction.

For me personally, I can testify that it is by this abundance of God's help that I have been able to prevail and reign in life! God's grace has become the means by which I live. I now lean and rely upon God in a way I never had before.

BE A GRACE GIVER

Pastors, come on, do you want your ministries to REIGN? Give your people an abundance of grace. Get rid of the lawyers. Get rid of the preachers of the letter. Many years ago, the Lord purged out of our church a group of preachers who were "of the letter" (2 Corinthians 3). Our church was immediately lifted into victorious liberty. We have walked and increased in this victory throughout the years.

Anyone of you can reign in life if you will receive this abundance of grace. My heart breaks to watch so many of you continue in your shame and struggle. You know God can set you free, but you refuse to believe He can do it by grace. Instead, you stubbornly struggle to free yourself. Consider the life you could have, the love you could have, the freedom you could have. But you forfeit the gift in an effort to earn it.

Do you want to encourage men? Give them an abundance of grace and the gift of righteousness. If you want to take the life out of them, if you want to defeat them, then tell them their salvation depends on their work; tell them they must perfect holiness in themselves.

I do not think I can speak too much of God's grace, for it is the means by which God himself has come to save me and is working in my life to accomplish everything He desires of me. Furthermore, if my relationship with God is on the basis of faith, then nothing can separate me from the love of God but unbelief! I have suffered the most horrendous blows of hell. The force and magnitude of hell has raged against my life. I have laid flat on my back as hell has launched its most powerful weapons against me. Lying there, broken, I would whisper, "Is that all you have? Your best has not separated me from the Love of God, which is in Christ Jesus my Lord."

The Lord told Paul that His grace was sufficient for him. Is it sufficient for you? When God chose the word sufficient, He was saying that my grace is able to lift you up; to take you up; to raise you; to carry you, and to free you.

The other evening I was riding home after a heavy day's work. I felt very wearied, and sore depressed, when swiftly, and suddenly as a lightning flash, that text came to me, "My grace is sufficient for thee." I reached home and looked it up in the original, and at last it came to me in this way, "MY grace is sufficient for thee"; and I said, "I should think it is, Lord," and burst out laughing. I never fully understood what the holy laughter of Abraham was until then. It seemed to make unbelief so absurd. It was as though some little fish, being very thirsty, was troubled about drinking the river dry, and Father Thames said, "Drink away, little fish, my stream is sufficient for thee." Or, it seemed after the seven years of plenty, a mouse feared it might die of famine; and Joseph might say, "Cheer up, little mouse, my granaries are sufficient for thee." Again, I imagined a man away up yonder, in a lofty mountain, saying to himself, "I breathe so many cubic feet of air every year. I fear I shall exhaust the oxygen in the atmosphere," but the earth might say, "Breathe away, O man, and fill the lungs ever, my atmosphere is sufficient for thee." Oh, brethren, be great believers! Little faith will bring your souls to Heaven, but great faith will bring Heaven to your souls. – C.H. Spurgeon.

Grace is associated with the power of God. And here is the tragedy of our day. Paul told Timothy that in the last days, men would have a form of godliness but deny the power thereof (2 Timothy 3). The power of godliness is grace. Multitudes deny this grace to believers everywhere.

Paul did not tell Timothy there would be a shortage of religion, a shortage of prayer, or a shortage of belief. He said they would deny the power. Beloved, I have watched the religious deny this power to their own destruction.

One of the greatest theologians in church history, A.B. Simpson, made this observation:

> A precious secret of the Christian life is to have Jesus dwelling within the heart and conquering things that we never could overcome. It is the only secret of power in your life and mine, beloved. Men cannot understand it, nor will the world believe it; but it is true, that God will come to dwell within us, and be the power, and the purity, and the victory, and the joy of our life. It is no longer now, "What is the best that I can do?" but the question is, "What is the best that Christ can do?" It enables us to say, with Paul, in that beautiful passage in Philippians, "I know both how to be abased, and I know how to abound, everywhere and in all things, I am instructed both to be full and to be hungry, both to abound and to suffer need. I can do all things through Christ, which strengthened me."
>
> With this knowledge I go forth to meet my testings, and the secret stands me good. It keeps me pure and sweet, as I could never keep myself. Christ has met the adversary and defeated him for me. Thanks be unto God who giveth us the victory through Jesus Christ. – A.B. Simpson

You can reign in life, living by grace through faith. I encourage you to receive the abundance of grace and the gift of righteousness. There is a faithful and good God who has given you the victory in Jesus.

Chapter 7
DON'T FAINT IN THE DAY OF TEMPTATION

You may be sitting in a world fallen apart wondering how any good can ever come out of this hell. You may be wondering how victory can come out of such defeat. It is not for you to know; it is for you to believe—to believe in the victory Christ has won for you!

I do not know how God does it. I have seen women lying in the hospital beds next to their suffering children whispering, "God shall bring us through this!" I have seen fathers breathlessly driving up to fatal accidents, shredding through bloody debris to hold their loved one in their arms. How do they come back from these moments? By believing, "I shall see the goodness of the Lord in the land of the living."

When you believe in seeing the goodness of the Lord in the land of the living, you have the faith to rise up above your troubles! Through faith you are able to walk in victory. You triumph by the hope you have in the goodness of God. You may not possess that good thing you are hoping for, but faith assures you, you shall.

What can you possibly give the man whose son lies dead from an overdose in his back bedroom? What do you possibly offer the man whose wife says, "I don't love you anymore. I want a divorce!" Is there victory for these people? What hope can possibly be given? These dear ones must be given the hope of a good God!

He is not only the God who is able to care for headaches, a chipped tooth, flat tires, or flight delays. He is the living, Almighty, good God. He reaches into the chasm of deep, dark despair and brings light. He walks into the despair of hospital rooms and triumphantly resurrects hope. He carries the abandoned man to hope again for love. He holds the man who is holding his deceased loved one. I don't know how God does it, but He does!

He is not a weak God. And you are not a flower, blown by the wind of affliction. Your life is not governed by your bad times or good times. Your life is in His hands! He is the God of the constellations, the God of the oceans, the God of the nations, the God of heaven, and the God of angels. He is God in the darkness. He is God in the light. He is God in the pain. He is God in the healing. He is still God at the grave! He is God in the courtroom. He is the God of here and the God of there! He is not weak!

UNLESS

It takes faith to triumph in this evil world, "Unless I had believed to see the goodness of the Lord in the land of the living ...!" Unless I had believed to see the goodness of the Lord in my life. UNLESS! There it is; you can either believe to see the goodness of the Lord in this life or you can just give up right now. Put the period to your life; it is over now.

The great message of Psalm 73 is this: when you have been through a season where your "steps had well nigh slipped," you can still come out with faith and victory. The Psalmist went into the presence of the Lord and warred against his temptations to envy the ungodly. Before God, he considered their eternal end. There, in God's presence, he made an end to these temptations that insinuated serving God was a waste of time. He was freed from temporal pressures and rejoiced that not only would he be with God forever, but that he would also see the goodness of the Lord in his present life.

You may be perplexed. Your faith may be hanging by a thread, but that does not matter as long as, at the end, you arrive on that great high plateau where you stand face to face with God, having an assurance you have not had before. You can make use of the devil and all his assaults, but you have to learn how to handle him.

In the presence of God, you can turn all of Satan's strategies into great spiritual victories. I was tempted to think there were times when it appeared God was not good to me; I see now that I was wrong. God is always good in all circumstances, in all ways, at all times—no matter what may happen to me or to anyone else.

CAN YOU BELIEVE?

I have arrived at the conclusion that God is always good. Are you ready to say that? Some of you may be passing through the kind of experience that causes you to question God and His goodness. Things may be going wrong with you, and you are facing very difficult calamities. Blow upon blow may be descending upon you. You have been living the Christian life, reading your Bible, working for God, and yet the blows have come, one on top of another. Everything seems to be going wrong. You have been plagued all day, chastened every morning. One trouble follows another.

Now the one simple question I want to ask is this: In the face of such miseries, are you able to say, "God is always good"? Can you believe even when you see the wicked flourish? In spite of the cruelty of an enemy or the treachery of a friend, in spite of all that is happening to you, can you say, "God is always good; there is no exception; there is no qualification?"

Can you say that? You may have been tempted to doubt. That is to be expected; that is not sin. The question is, were you able to overcome the temptation to doubt God? Were you able to resist the devil? Were you able to put on the mind of Christ?

The Bible is written for believers to be victorious—to win and overcome. Its stories are filled with examples of failing men and women who rely on an unfailing God. The only means of winning is faith! You must overcome: the world, what you hear, and what you see by faith! John said whatever is born of God overcomes the world: and this is the victory that overcomes the world—our faith. He that believes Jesus is the Son of God overcomes the world (1 John 5:4–5). And to overcome the world is to overcome the god of this world, the lies of this world, the condemnation of this world, the depression of this world, the hell of this world, and the heartache of this world.

FAITH IS REQUIRED

Nothing requires more faith than the faith to believe you are not defeated when it seems as though you are. Nothing requires more faith than to believe you are not forsaken when it seems as though you are. Nothing requires more faith than to believe your good days are going to come when all of your dreams have just been laid to rest.

Paul looked defeated under a pile of stones. He was acquainted with trouble, perplexity, and persecution. He was cast down, but he could victoriously say through faith that he was not destroyed (2 Corinthians 4).

Believing to see God's goodness is the means of winning after denying and cursing the Lord or falling into immorality and murder. Faith in the goodness of God causes you to rise from the fall and hope for the good that God can bring from all of this. David cried, "Purge me with hyssop, and I shall be clean: wash me, and I shall be whiter than snow. Make me to hear joy and gladness; that the bones which thou hast broken may rejoice. Hide thy face from my sins, and blot out all mine iniquities. Create in me a clean heart, O God; and renew a right spirit within me. Restore unto me the joy of thy salvation; and uphold me with thy free spirit" (Psalm 51:7–12).

All victors rose by faith in the goodness of God to claim the victory! Perhaps you have considered yourself lost. You have not exercised faith; and therefore, you are done. You are one of the defeated ones. Beloved, do you know why Satan is still fighting you? It is because you are not defeated yet. He may be kicking you. The devil may be gloating but rise up in faith. You shall beat that dragon! Maybe you have not displayed the best attitude at all times. The fact is, you wanted to quit but you have not! You are still overcoming.

DO YOU REALLY WANT TO GIVE UP HERE?

Defeat is unbelief! It is to give up on God! Do you understand what I am telling you? I am saying that if you can believe that God can still be God here, in this place, then you can still claim the victory! Understand, I am not asking you to know how God can. I am not even asking if you can see how it is possible. I am only asking if you believe God can be God—here.

Sometimes life gets so tough that even the most faith-filled Christian has difficulty summoning the faith to pray for a breakthrough. A difficult problem or a heart-breaking set of circumstances can suddenly seem too massive to move. We must always be certain of the following: First, no situation is beyond the scope of prayer because God can do anything. We must pray and wait. And second, though we may affirm the truth of scripture, we must learn to lean on the promises and not give way to worry, murmuring, or complaining.

> Hast thou not known? Hast thou not heard, that the everlasting God, the Lord, the Creator of the ends of the earth, fainteth not, neither is weary? There is no searching of His understanding. He giveth power to the faint; and to them that have no might He increaseth strength. Even the youths shall faint and be weary, and the young men shall utterly fall: But they that wait upon the Lord shall renew their strength; they shall mount up with wings as eagles; they shall run, and not be weary; and they shall walk, and not faint (Isaiah 40: 28–31).

Don't faint, beloved, you are not of those who throw away your confidence and go back to perdition. You are a believer and you believe to the saving of your souls (Hebrews 10).

Even Jesus wrestled with troubles: "Now is my soul troubled …" (John 12: 27). Fiery darts were filling the spiritual night; the tranquility of His soul was broken. In Gethsemane, Jesus taught us to fight back by believing God. We do not look at Gethsemane and justify our depression, but we see how it should be fought!

Notice what Jesus did that night of trouble. He chose close friends to be with Him and join Him in prayer. He opened His soul to them. He asked for their help by way of interceding with Him. His hope was not in His friends. His hope was set upon His Father. He trusted and rested in His Father's wisdom and will. He fixed His eyes upon the future. For the joy set before Him, He endured the cross, despising the shame. He now sits enthroned with His Father on the throne of heaven!

Likewise, beloved, you can never be a demonstration of His life and overcome hell if you faint whenever adversity strikes! I can promise, God will not fail, and neither shall your faith! You shall rise if you will endure through faith. You are about to see the goodness of God!

The eternal essence of a thing or a circumstance is not in the thing itself but in one's reaction to it. The distressing situation will pass, but one's reaction to it results in a permanent moral and spiritual deposit in the character. Satan intends that adversity shall drive one away from God, causing him to sit in judgment upon Him, to question His motives, His goodness, and justice.

Satan slanders God by suggesting that God has mistreated one, and that if He was really all-good and all-powerful HE would never allow this sorrow or calamity to come to any of His children.

When one allows the misfortune, affliction, or sorrow to drive him to God, the effect is just the opposite. Accepting the seeming misfortune as from the hand of an All-wise, All-loving, and All-powerful God, who always works all things together for the good of the beloved, and praising Him that nothing intrinsically evil can ever come to the one of His children is a reaction that strengthens and reinforces all that is best and most godlike in character.

With this reaction God's purpose is achieved and Satan has lost. The adversity has left the individual stronger in faith, courage, and knowledge of God. A God who can take all evil and by His divine grace so transform them that they boomerang against Satan, enhance the character of the saint, and redound to the glory of God, is worthy of unceasing praise. – Amy Carmichael

Chapter 8
I ALMOST FAINTED

It just seems like you are going down, but down is the way up! "Up" is the way the Holy Spirit led Jesus (Matthew 4:1). From His anointing in the Jordan River, the Holy Spirit led Jesus up! But do notice: He was led by the Spirit up into the wilderness! The wilderness is a desert place—a barren place. Is it possible that the Holy Spirit will lead you into seasons of dryness, of barrenness? Of course He will! And why did the Spirit lead Jesus up into the wilderness? He led Jesus up into the wilderness to be tempted of the devil!

You are God's child! You are God's possession; you are not going down: down in defeat, down in despair. You are going up, even when it looks like you are going down! You may be fighting hell right now, but you are going up! You may be afflicted with depression and confusion, but you are going up. You may be walking through the valley of the shadow of death, but you are going up! You are God's redeemed and you are ascending. It doesn't matter how hard times are, how confusing your circumstances are—you are going up! It doesn't matter how often you get knocked down by the enemy—you are getting up! You may have fallen in sin, but the righteous man gets UP seven times (Proverbs 24:16)! Do not allow a mystery to separate you from the love of God! Do not let seasons of confusion rob you of your faith! Refuse to let the enemy bring you down when the Holy Spirit wants to bring you up!

Consider the circumstances of Psalms 27: Evil doers…adversaries…a host against me…war against me…the day of trouble…mine enemies round about me…my father and my mother have forsaken me…false witnesses…people breathing out cruelties against me! This is coming from a man who God personally raised, anointed, and joined Himself to—King David!

But also consider the affirmation of David: My heart will not be afraid. I will be confident. Mine head shall be lifted up. I will sing! Why? Because I had fainted unless I believed to see the goodness of the Lord in the land of the living (Psalms 27:13)! Our God is the Lord of goodness!

He is the Lord of all that is right, all that is beautiful, all that is glad, and all that makes for the true prosperity of human life. He is the Lord of goodness, for He is the fountainhead from which all these things proceed and the means by which these things become real in the experience of life down here below.

So what effect is this to have on you, this fact that God is the Lord of goodness? What is the light David is giving to those of you who inhabit this strange, weird life of yours? How does it help you? In what sense does belief in this God turn *the sighing into song, the fear into faith, the sorrow into joy?*

Life itself, whatever mystery you may have to face, whatever pain you may have to endure, whatever darkness you may have to go through, whatever agony you may have to bear, whatever sins you may have to mourn, is vast, immeasurable, and unforeseeable. Life seems to be so inconsistent; therefore, you need an anchor of hope. To this very God of goodness, you must fling all your hope! It is to this God, who has measured the length of your days, ordered your steps, and planned for your glorious ending—that all your experiences must be measured and directed. It is then, and only then, that the unbearable moments and crushing pains of life take on a new meaning, a new value.

Are you disappointed with yourself? This disappointment can also reveal the goodness of the Lord. He has put inside of you greater things than that which you are experiencing. He is lifting you to greater causes and purposes. He is not giving you disappointment to depress you; He is leading you up through the strange disappointments to accomplish things of eternal value.

The goodness of the Lord in the land of the living is that which makes a man, broken and disappointed with himself, look up into the Face of God and resolutely and daringly say, "Thou wilt perfect that which concerneth me." If you take that hope away, then you shall despair in the midst of life!

LIFE IS NOT A TRAGEDY

When you believe to see the goodness of the Lord in the land of the living, *you have the faith to rise up above your troubles! This faith reckons upon the fact that nothing is hidden from the Lord.* What you know not, He knows. What amazes you never amazes Him!

I am not surprised that men who lose their faith in God, who go down into depression, and sink into the despair of life, seek to end their lives. It takes faith to triumph in this evil world, "Unless I had believed to see the goodness of the Lord in the land of the living …!" (Psalm 27:13) Without that faith, life is not worthwhile; life is a tragedy.

Blot out this God from the heavens, deny me the Face of God that shines in merciful tenderness upon my pain, take this God of the Bible away from me, then life is some hideous mockery and the sport of demons.

Unless I had believed to see the goodness of the Lord in my life—UNLESS! Oh, the horror of it, the sheer horror of the tragedy—I would have FAINTED! This fainting is not what you may think. It is not the fainting you are familiar with. Of course, it would imply that the hope of living is gone, and the man who cannot believe to see good in his life may seek to end his life. But another fainting is possible—the fainting of doing what is right: giving up and becoming a rebel. The soul would become red-hot, quick and alive with agony and despair, challenge and revolt, hot anger and rebellion.

Rebellion against what? Rebellion against the tragedy of being born. Rebellion against God for making me weak, rebellion against life for disappointing me, rebellion against everything and everyone just because—just because of the mystery, the sin, and the death—the whole dark outlook of life. God will be blamed. He usually is. But He is not at fault. He wants to lead you "up." However, it is not His fault if you refuse to be led of the Holy Spirit.

THE GREATEST OF MEN STRUGGLE WITH LIFE

In Psalm 73, the Psalmist confesses he was in such a rebellious place. His feet were almost gone, his steps had well-nigh slipped ... he was like a beast before God. I know of nothing in the spiritual life more discouraging than to meet the kind of person who seems to give the impression that he or she is always walking on the mountain top. That is certainly not true in the Bible. The Bible tells us that these men and women knew what it was to be cast down and to be in sore and grievous trouble.

Notice that in the Psalm, he starts off with a great triumphant note, "Truly God is good to Israel, even to such as are of a clean heart." The Psalmist is giving a testimony, "Now I am going to tell you a story. I am going to tell you what has happened to me; but the thing I want to leave with you is just this—the goodness of God." He starts with the end; and then he proceeds to tell us how he got there. He shares that he was very badly shaken and that he very nearly fell. What was the cause of his trouble? Simply that he did not understand God's way with respect to him.

He had become aware of a painful fact. Here he was living a godly life; he was cleansing his heart—washing his hands in innocency. He was practicing the godly life, avoiding sin, meditating upon the things of God, and spending his time in prayer. He was in the habit of examining his life, and whenever he found sin he confessed it to God with sorrow, seeking forgiveness and renewal. The man was devoting himself to a life which would be pleasing in God's sight. He kept clear of the world and its polluting effects. He separated himself from evil works. He gave himself up to living this godly life. Yet, although he was doing all this, he was having a great deal of trouble, "... all the day long have I been plagued, and chastened every morning." He was having a difficult time reconciling why his life, devoted to God, was filled with such peril.

The Psalmist does not tell us exactly what was happening; it may have been illness or trouble in his family. He was being tried, and tried very sorely. In fact, everything seemed to be going wrong and nothing seemed to be going right. However, the ungodly seemed to get away with everything. The ungodly prospered! The ungodly did not fight this hell that the godly had to fight! In other words, why does the Spirit lead us UP into the wilderness to be tempted of the devil?

The Psalmist believed God to be holy and righteous and true. He believed God was One who intervenes on behalf of His people and surrounds them with loving care and wonderful promises. His problem was how to reconcile all this with what was happening to him and what was happening to the ungodly.

PERPLEXITY IS NOT SURPRISING

It is often thought that God should be blessing His own children always and that they should never be chastised. How often have you thought that? You think, "Why doesn't God wipe out my enemies? Why does God not mock the wicked who mock God? Why does He not make a of show of their arrogance?"

God's mind is eternal. God's ways are so infinitely above yours that you must always assume that you are not going to understand everything He does. If you approach life as though everything should always be plain and clear, you shall soon find yourself in the place where the Psalmist found himself: your feet almost slipping, on the verge of fainting. It is not surprising that when you look into the mind of the Eternal, there should be times when you are given the impression that things are working out in a manner exactly opposite to what you think they ought to be.

PERPLEXITY IS NOT SINFUL

There are those who give the impression that they think the ways of God are always perfectly plain and clear. They always seem to be able to reason thus: the sky is always bright and shining, and we are always perfectly happy. Well, all I can say is that they are absolutely superior to Paul (2 Corinthians 4).

Yes, it is wrong to be in a state of despair; but it is not wrong to be perplexed. The mere fact that you may be perplexed about something that is happening at the present time does not mean you are guilty of sin. You are in God's hand, and yet something unpleasant is happening to you. You say, "I do not understand." There is nothing wrong with that. To be perplexed is not sinful. Your mind is finite. It is also weakened by sin. You do not see things clearly. You do not know what is best for you; therefore, it is natural to be perplexed.

PERPLEXITY OPENS THE DOOR TO TEMPTATION

Temptation is so powerful that it shakes the greatest and strongest saint. Temptation does indeed get you down, you may say, as the Psalmist, "As for me ... my feet were almost gone; my steps had well-nigh slipped" (Psalm 73:2).

Perhaps you reason, "But that was the Old Testament and the Holy Spirit had not come as He has come now. I am in the Christian position, whereas this saint of God who wrote the Psalm was not in the New Covenant." This argument fails, however, when you read the words of Paul. In explaining the Christian position to the Corinthians, Paul goes back into the Old Testament for an illustration. And lest some of those superior people in Corinth might say, "We have received the Holy Spirit; we are not like that," Paul says, "Wherefore let him that thinketh he standeth take heed lest he fall" (1 Corinthians 10:12).

Temptation comes as a veritable hurricane, causing havoc to everything in its path. Temptation can possess such terrific might that even a man of God is practically overwhelmed. Such is the power of temptation! There is nothing stronger about temptation than the way in which, under its influence and power, godly people consider doing things that in normal conditions would be quite unthinkable.

The Psalmist said, "I was envious of the foolish!" He was envious of the arrogant. The Psalmist is saying that he can hardly put it on paper; he is so heartily ashamed of it. But I have to confess that there was a moment when I was envious of ungodly people. Only the blinding effect of temptation can explain that. Temptation comes with such force that we are knocked off our balance and are no longer able to think clearly. It always comes with that intention.

DEFEATING TEMPTATION

Now, there is nothing more vital in this spiritual warfare than for you to realize you can actually face a temptation that is designed to make you faint. Therefore, you cannot afford to relax your faith for one moment. Satan will wield his temptations in an effort to make you see only what he wants you to see.

He wants you to question God. He wants you to complain when the Holy Spirit leads you up into wildernesses to be tempted of the devil. He wants you to forget eternity and live for the temporal happiness the world can afford. He wants you to accuse God by making you think God has withheld good things from you. He wants you to curse God and become a rebel, full of bitterness toward the God you once loved. This is the blinding effect of temptation. And if you think you would never fall for such a temptation, the Apostle Paul tries to warn you, "Wherefore let him that thinketh he standeth take heed lest he fall" (1 Corinthians 10:12).

Just look at you. Keeping your heart clean. Keeping your hands clean. Spending all your time denying yourself. You believe the gospel, but just look what has happened to you since you believed! Life is more difficult! If God loves you, why are you having such a hard time? Why would God deal with you like this? My friend, you are making a mistake; you are doing yourself grievous damage and harm; you are not fair to yourself! Why do you serve a God who has the power to do so much for you, yet He does not? Why do you not curse God and die? These are the grievous accusations of temptation.

BEWARE OF TEMPTATION'S LOGIC

Temptation has logic; this is where it possesses so much power. However, its logic is something like this: "Go ahead, eat the apple for all of its benefits even though you will lose your soul at the end." Jesus attacked this tempting lie when He said, "What does it matter if you gain the whole world but lose your soul." It is temporarily pleasing, but eternally foolish. Just look at the Psalmist. He is confused. Why is it that those who are striving to live a holy life, a godly life, are suffering more than those who have no regard for God? Why do the ungodly prosper? This just doesn't seem fair.

Other men are blaspheming God, and with lofty utterances are saying things which should never be thought, let alone said. Yet, they are prosperous; their children are all doing well; they have more than the heart could desire. Meanwhile, you are suffering the exact opposite. There is only one conclusion to draw—looking at it from the human view, why should you continue serving God? If temptation never provided this logic, then there would be no temptation.

DO NOT GIVE TEMPTATION POWER

There is no sin in temptation. Do not fall into condemnation because you have been tempted. Jesus was tempted, but He sinned not. Do not allow Satan to manipulate you with the guilt of sin. Thoughts are always put to you, and they are not sin. This knowledge is crucial to winning the battle over temptation and moving up in the Holy Ghost. You must learn to draw a distinction between being tempted and sinning.

You cannot control the thoughts put in your mind by the devil. Paul talks of the fiery darts. With the Psalmist, the devil was hurling the thoughts at him. Even the Lord was tempted. But, if you welcome such thoughts and AGREE with them, then they become sin.

Chapter 9
WHEN THE SHAME BECOMES GLORY

"And the angel answered and said unto her, The Holy Ghost shall come upon thee, and the power of the Highest shall overshadow thee: therefore, also that holy thing which shall be born of thee shall be called the Son of God" (Luke 1:35).

In contemplating the birth of Jesus ... pondering the miracle of His incarnation, I marvel how God moved upon Mary by the Holy Ghost and placed within her the life of Jesus—the Word eternal, living inside of her being. I am honestly stunned by the glory of God.

For nine months, what she carried would be so vague. The only thing she could do was hide everything in her heart. It was beyond her ability to explain what God was doing inside of her life. It was beyond her ability to even grasp it herself. She could make no sense of it, but she could feel it; it had her! She could not escape what God was doing. Wherever she would run, wherever she would go, whatever she would do, she could not escape this move of God. And because it was the Eternal Word that was placed inside of her, there came a point in her life when she could not hide it. The thing she hid in her heart now became very evident in her life. For that Word began to manifest Himself through her as well as in her.

Only when the fullness of time had come, when the fullness of life was accomplished, only then was that which was in her allowed to come forth and affect the nations. But His life would not come forth prematurely. Not until that life of Christ had been fully formed first within her would that life of Christ come forth from her. But notice; it was not a mature Christ that came out of her—He was a baby! However, He was fully formed and able to be sustained in a world that would seek His demise. Not until the fullness of His time would He be born; only then would that life of Christ come forth from her—a life to be manifested among the nations as a light to the world and the Savior of mankind. And though He was an infant, He was Jesus!

Many of you reading this have experienced the Holy Ghost moving within your life. Obviously, this word in you is not the same as Mary's Word in her. Nonetheless, the word has been placed within you. You cannot explain it, you cannot grasp it, you cannot define it, and you cannot get your mind around it.

As Mary lived nine months in public shame and humility, even into her adult life, some also misunderstand you in the midst of your own confusion as to what God is doing with you. So much in life does not make sense. Obviously, there is so much about you that does not make sense. And the thing is, you can't explain it because you can't get your mind around it. Like Mary, you just hide it in your heart.

But that life will grow, that word will grow, it will increase, and before long it will begin to manifest itself in your life. Then, in the fullness of time, when Jesus is formed within you, will that life come forth to affect the nations. It is the Life of God that is to come forth—not theologies, not doctrines, not right or wrong, but Jesus Himself: His life, His personality formed within you. And not until He is fully formed within you will He be able to come forth from you to affect the nations.

DON'T ABORT YOUR LIFE

Beloved, labor to bring forth this life. Go through the agony, the confusion. Let His life grow in you. Let His word take hold of you. Believe in the power of the Holy Spirit to do this work. To bring forth this life into the world, you need more than a move of the Spirit. You need anticipation that the Spirit will do it. Anticipate that the confusion of your life will become clear, that the pain of your life will become prosperous, and that the shame of your life will become Glory! Amen!

The Holy Ghost came upon Mary. He overshadowed her and changed the world! The answer to everything in your life: your family, your society, and the world is that the Holy Spirit would overshadow you. That He would come upon you with power—putting the Word of God into your being to birth out from you things only His Spirit could produce. Imagine the Holy Spirit bringing something out of you that will turn the world upside-down. Can you believe it? Is He not able?

You see, so many can only believe that their effectiveness for God is based on their education, their experience, and their tenure in being a Christian. They mistakenly consider that the ministers of God's Kingdom are those that man, institutions, and time have produced. But God considers His ministers to be those individuals in whom the Life of His Son is being formed—those in whom Jesus has become so great that He comes forth from them into their world.

YOU MUST CONSENT TO GOD'S WILL

This anointing, the overshadowing of the Holy Ghost, is not automatic. Mary had to consent, "Be it done unto me according to Your Word." You must live by faith on this new basis of God's dealings with you, or you will miss the divine life intended.

Oh, how wonderful is the Holy Ghost to come and put the Life of God into our being! In Genesis 1, He moved upon the desolate earth and in six days brought forth the beauty of creation. If we will, the Holy Ghost will come upon us and impregnate us with the purposes of God. He will fill us; He will give life to our spirit.

Whatever you have acquired, the knowledge you have learned or qualifications you have gained means nothing to the Work of God if it has not come to you by the Holy Ghost. God is pleased with His Son. The value of your life and service is measured only by the extent to which you have allowed the Holy Ghost to form Jesus within you.

- Everything That Is Eternal Is The Work Of The Holy Spirit.
- Every Relevant Work Of God Is By The Spirit.
- Every Miracle Is By The Spirit.
- Every Impossibility Becomes Possible By The Spirit.
- He Is The Creator Of Eternal Conditions.
- He Is The Creator Of The Conditions Of Revival.
- He Is The Witness Of The Lord Jesus Christ.

He Is the Power of Resurrection—He alone has the power to restore the life that men and sin took from you. He can raise you from despair ... release you from prison ... bring you back from death and defeat all your enemies! He can anoint you. He alone knows your creative purposes and how to fulfill them.

BEWARE OF MEN

Because your life is a work of the Spirit, and He alone knows what He is doing and can sustain that work within you and can produce the purposes of God through you, you must beware of man and yourself!

Who could have counseled Mary? What human had experience with a pregnant virgin to help her understand what was going on in her life? Mary had to press in close to the Lord and trust Him.

The angel said the Holy Ghost was going to do something with her. Now she must wait in faith for Him to perform His Word. No one, not even you, can understand the full purposes of God for your life. You must trust what God is doing with you. Christian counsel is beneficial, but sometimes no one can explain what God is doing with you. You must hold that Word inside of you until it is time for the birth! Who can trace the way of God? His path is in the sea. "Thy way is in the sea, and thy path in the great waters, and thy footsteps are not known" (Psalms 77:19). Have faith in the Lord, and if you consent to His desires for your life, then get ready. You are about to have a life-changing experience!

LET GOD NAME YOU

Mary did not understand everything about Jesus. She did not grasp the full significance of His life. She could not possibly comprehend all He would suffer and accomplish. God alone knew these things; therefore, God named His Son. God gave Jesus His name because His name would signify His destiny!

The pages of history are marked by men and women who have learned their God-given names. It is interesting to imagine how many new names God will have to give out in Glory, possibly signifying how many people lived the destiny that others set for them but not the destiny God had desired. Just consider the names given to Elisha: a farmer, a servant to the prophet. Never was he regarded as more than someone inferior to the great men of his day. But Elisha knew what God put in him. He held that in faith, knowing his day would come. All those years behind the oxen and caring for the prophet were the years in which the Lord was producing something within him, and he knew this life would come forth in time.

WHEN GOD IS SILENT

Have faith in the Lord. If you consent to His desires for your life, then don't allow your confusion and God's silence to define your destiny. There are times when the only thing you can do is stand on the last thing you know you heard from God. What do you do in the confusion? Well, if you move on your own, outside of God's word already given to you, then you can get the faith beaten out of you.

Satan will come to you in this confusion and tell you what a loser you are. Satan will suggest, "You are crazy. Did God say …?" Satan will take the life out of you. He will seek to abort what God is creating. Satan will fix your eyes upon present-day life.

If Satan is telling you, "Did God say …?" then perhaps God did say! Also, if Satan is trying to discourage you and make you feel worthless, then it is a good sign that something supernatural is happening in you. You see, most of the time Satan wants you to live in pride so God will resist you. But when you are feeling worthless, unworthy of God, and disqualified for the Lord's purposes in your life, then that is probably the work of the Holy Ghost, not Satan. It is the work of the Holy Spirit because He is causing your self-reliance to decrease so that the Lord Jesus' life in you might increase. He is humbling you and making you desperate for the Lord's anointing in your life.

Another alternative when you are in a season of confusion is to live by the Word of God, like Mary. Not only did she hide these things in her heart, but she also pondered them! You must preach to yourself and preach faith to yourself—refuse to look or listen to anything that will weaken your faith. Furthermore, stand and do the last thing you know God told you to do. Don't live by what you see, the place you are in, or the conditions that seem inescapable because what you see is not accurate, where you are is not permanent, and your conditions are not a hindrance to the victory.

DON'T LET THE PAIN STOP THE BIRTH

Have faith in the Lord. If you consent to His desires for your life, then there will come a time when the pain is unbearable, and you have to push that life out. No one else can give birth to the life in you but you! God put that life in you, and you must exercise the faith to live the life God has called you to. The men and women who by faith acted upon God's will are the ones who have affected the generations for God. If you ever wonder how in the world God could use you to change the world, then take a look at those in the Bible who pushed out the life God put within them. One great example is Peter. Who is that preaching on Pentecost? Who is accusing the people of denying Jesus? The very one who denied Him! Peter! When the Holy Ghost reached into that room for a preacher, he didn't grab John; He grabbed Peter, the denier!

Time would fail me to mention David, Moses, Sarah, Abraham, and innumerable others who, throughout history, simply believed God could do something through their worthless lives. If they lived for people, then they would have been swallowed up in history. But because they lived for God, they were the ones who made history!

Wherever you are, whatever you have done, regardless of your feelings or the devil's condemnations, get up. Get over it. Get to Jesus. Let God put something inside of you. Start now! Live for God. Don't live by what you see or feel; live by the God you know!

Don't live by what people have called you: worthless, stupid, fake, hypocrite. What is the name that God wants to give you? What is the destiny God has for you? I can assure you of this: it will constitute the fact that you are mighty in Christ and more than a conqueror. No longer will you be the defeated and cast-down poor soul everybody feels sorry for. You will be God's! Your life will affect the nations!

Chapter 10
THE INSANITY OF PAUL

I wish I could write this next scripture slowly because I know your tendency is to read it quickly! This was not intended to be read quickly. It is filled with emotion. It is a Messianic psalm capturing the heart of the Messiah as only the Holy Spirit can convey. Be still as you read. Be quiet! Listen. Feel the words. These words are meant for you! Though they are cried to the Father, they were intended for you to feel them. Jesus is concerned that you will be offended in Him. Here it is.

> Let not them that wait on thee, O Lord God of hosts, be ashamed for my sake: let not those that seek thee be confounded for my sake, O God of Israel. Because for thy sake I have borne reproach; shame hath covered my face. I am become a stranger unto my brethren, and an alien unto my mother's children. For the zeal of thine house hath eaten me up; and the reproaches of them that reproached thee are fallen upon me (Psalms 69:6–9).

There you go ... reading it fast! But wait! Listen to Jesus' cry. Feel His passion, this zeal that is eating Him up. Here, Jesus is depicted as being drenched in shame! He feels the shame. He can imagine the multitudes that will not understand how someone so loathsome can be the One upon which all men should hope!

Allow me some liberty as I paraphrase Jesus' concern here:

> Oh Father, please don't let those who are waiting for you, waiting for your promised Messiah, be ashamed of You when they see me. Please, Father, don't let those who are seeking You be confused by the shame I will go through. When they see me on the cross—naked, rejected, hated, despised, defecating on myself, helpless—please, Father, don't let them be confused and turn away!
>
> Please hear me, Father! Turn to me in Your mercies. Don't hide Your face from me. You know my reproach, my shame, and my dishonor. You see all of my enemies surrounding my cross and hating me. Please, Father, don't You turn also!
>
> My heart breaks from the reproach. I am full of heaviness. I looked for someone who would have pity on me. Surely, someone in heaven or on earth would have pity for me, but no one did! I had no comforter (Psalms 69:16–21).

But the zeal for the Lord's house consumed Him. He went forth and tread the winepress alone. He bore for us the fury of God's wrath against sin. Why did He do this? For the House of God! So that the Father could have His Church! So that the shamed sinners can have freedom from their shame! Hebrews 12:2 captures this. "... for the joy that was set before Him [He] endured the cross, despising the shame ..." Jesus despised the shame. This means that Jesus looked down upon the shame. Jesus attributed no worth or influence to shame; He treated it as an outcast. It was simply not an issue to Him. In other words, the opinions and judgments of the self-righteous leaders would not intimidate His zeal to free the shamed and oppressed. He refused to allow their opinions to affect Him. He refused to defend Himself against their accusations so that they would like Him. Therefore, He could prefer the company of outcasts. He could touch the unclean and not care what holy people would think of Him. He could wash someone's feet. He could touch lepers. He could allow prostitutes to cling to Him. He could defend the outcast from religious brutality! He could take a cross and publicly die! Actually, this was the height of shame and dishonor—dying on a Roman cross. And Jesus suffered it all!

Just consider how the world changed when Jesus came. Unclean people were filled with hope. The shamed were set free and boldly went out to follow Jesus. When they saw him, they felt compelled to touch him because they understood that their salvation was near. They came alive!

Consider also the surge of hope that filled the atmosphere when they heard that Jesus was near. Consider how they rose from their filth to touch hope! Consider how unstoppable they were when the cure to their disease was at hand! Don't get in the way of someone who is both desperate and hopeful when the King is near. Jesus was an outcast, and the outcast knew He could heal them. Therefore, what is this shame Jesus despised? He despised the oppression of sin and its power over humanity. He despised the addiction that imprisoned so many. He despised the shame of divorce and broken relationships. He despised the diseases that caused multitudes to hide from family and friends. He despised the humiliation that covered men and women.

He did not create you to be covered with this shame! Therefore, He clothed Himself in that shame, in that reproach, in order that He could remove it from all men and clothe them in His glory! For Jesus, honor before God outweighs whatever shame you experience before mere creatures!

FEW COMFORTERS

Jesus is still despised today. Very few are His comforters. Very few are those who have pity on Him. Just imagine how insane a person who actively sought to recruit others to follow someone who was crucified on a Roman cross would appear to the world. This is just what the author of Hebrews is doing! This has to be insanity: "Wherefore Jesus also, that He might sanctify the people with His own blood, suffered without the gate. Let us go forth therefore unto Him without the camp, bearing His reproach" (Hebrews 13:12–13).

Take a moment to consider the historical shame of crucifixion. Before crucifying their victims, the Romans tortured them. From Plato, Republic II: 361d-362a, the Romans would *"...have to endure* the lash, the rack, chains, the branding-iron in his eyes, and finally, after every extremity of suffering, he will be crucified…"; thus, began the degrading loss of all dignity.

So, dear shamed one, do you feel exposed, embarrassed around good people? Jesus understands your shame. It was out of this that Jesus cried, (a paraphrase) "Father, please don't let those who are looking for You be ashamed or embarrassed and confused because of me. It is for You that I am covered in disgrace and shame!"

Crucifixion was designed to humiliate the person. The person was stripped naked before being hung on a cross so that his genitals would be publicly exposed. Obviously, the Romans sought to humiliate their victims. Crowds would gather around the grisly sight. His mother, His sisters, His brothers were all there looking on at that sight! As the victim drew near to expiring on the cross, his bowels would loosen, causing him to defecate and urinate on himself.

Crucifixion was a horrid picture on the Roman landscape, and it was intended to be. Cicero argued that Roman citizens should not ever have to hear the word "cross." He said: *"Even if death be threatened, we may die free men; but the executioner, and the veiling of the head, and the mere name of the cross, should be far removed, not only from the persons of Roman citizens—from their thoughts, and eyes, and ears. For not only the actual fact and endurance of all these things, but the bare possibility of being exposed to them —the expectation, the mere mention of them even —is unworthy of a Roman citizen and of a free man."*

And at the ghastly sight, Mark records: "They all left him and fled" (Mark 14:50). The crucifixion was a devastating blow to His disciples! Surely, this is why many of them abandoned Jesus and scattered after the crucifixion. They simply couldn't connect this kind of humiliation with glory, divinity, and triumph. Jesus was humiliated, shamed, and brutalized.

There was no comforter. There was no pity for Him. Why? Why did they leave? Because He was shame! His cross was shame! By the time Jesus got to the cross, you could count on one hand the number of people who were willing to be associated with him.

The Son of God, while on a rescue mission of love, was misunderstood, insulted, betrayed, denied, mocked, spit upon, cursed, abandoned, stripped, and crucified. And everybody fled from Him!

But wait! One comes…what is this insanity? What does he dare say? Is he actually declaring that One who died on a cross is, in fact, God? Who is this preaching the cross? Who is this making so much commotion about the Cross of Jesus? What insane person is embracing this event with such joy? Is it Saul of Tarsus? Dare he jeopardize so much reputation and accomplishment to glory in the cross?

Yes! Yes, he will! "… God forbid that I should glory, save in the cross of our Lord Jesus Christ …" (Galatians 6:14). He found in this cross freedom! Paul saw it. He saw the glory of Jesus. It was lowliness (Philippians 2:3). It was in esteeming others better than himself. Jesus had elevated the lowly by surrendering all to the One who is most lofty! It was not the approval of the mighty that Jesus was after. It was not the approval of the undefiled and religious that Jesus was after. Oh no, it was there … in the streets, among the broken and rejected—where Jesus would delight the Father's heart.

GLORYING IN THE CROSS

Jesus made Himself nothing in the world's eyes and Paul wants to do the same. Paul wants to imitate the shamed King and embrace being nothing before the world. Paul strove to become lowly in the world's eyes and was unaffected by the world's rejection. He counted all of his accomplishments as dung in comparison to the wealth of knowing Jesus! His churches were embarrassed of him! He boasted only in his weakness and suffering. He went around telling everyone he was the greatest sinner in a day when all wanted to be seen as holy. He went around promoting himself as the slave of the One who died on a cross!

He suffered rejection, insults, mockery, imprisonment, and beatings. Paul made the Cross the center of his theology in a day when the cross was the most shameful form of execution on earth! As Jesus, Paul was going to welcome shame, and boast in it by glorying in the Cross!

Individuals everywhere are trying to save their lives and reputations. They are trying to save themselves from pain, yet all the while they are dying at the hands of men. But those who have chosen the way of the crucified are free. They have nothing to defend. They have laid down their lives; therefore, what can man do to them?

Paul, defamed and crucified by his own people, beaten and crucified by the secular world, betrayed and crucified by professing believers, enduring innuendos, lies, attacks, false reports, beatings, plots, setbacks, failures, and even the destruction of his work, still rose from the grave of abuse and hate to show men the love of God.

His churches were nearly destroyed by men who professed to follow Jesus. His converts were nearly robbed of their grace by the deceitfulness of lawyers. Like David with Absalom, Paul took it all from the hand of God. He ran from none of it, altered none of it, yielded to all of it! His crucified life has literally saved the lives of innumerable believers because he triumphed in crucifixion and rose from the beating. He was not cynical. He was not hard. His crucifixion was voluntary—he chose this cross! He really loved.

To glory in the cross is the decision to surrender your will to God's. It is the decision to grasp the hand of God and agree to rejection from friends and family. It is to welcome the hammer, the nails, and the cross. It is the decision to have your family, your friends, or your church stare at you in horror, wondering what horrible thing you must have done.

You would bear it all. You would drink the cup, feel the shame, and become an object of humiliation and scorn. You would take pain as a crown, rejection as a throne, and humiliation as a royal robe worthy of wearing! You would be draped in the identity of another, having lost your own to this cross. You would see yourself in your Father's eyes and hear your worth from your Father's mouth, rather than the belligerent rants of the brutish crowds gathered to watch you die. You would agree to the lies and rumors that will continue to live long after you have died.

THRIVING IN SHAME

Are you a Christian? Are you a minister of the gospel? Do you boast in the Cross? Then don't be ashamed to embrace the shamed! Don't hide yourself from those men who have been deemed unworthy. When you make a feast, call the poor, the maimed, the lame, and the blind! Go out into the highways and hedges and compel all to come to the table.

Maybe this is why so many are lost, why so many shamed are dying in their shame. Perhaps it is because there are still so many who fail to comfort Jesus. So few are willing to go outside the camp and bear His reproach. So few are willing to demonstrate His message. They are too ashamed of people of shame, too scared to be an object of shame by the religious elite.

Luther was not afraid of going to Jesus. Luther's good friend George Spalatin was a pastor who had made a scandalous error. In response, Luther said:

> Therefore, my faithful request and admonition is that you join our company and associate with us, who are real, great, and hard-boiled sinners. You must by no means make Christ to seem paltry and trifling to us, as though He could be our Helper only when we want to be rid from imaginary, nominal, and childish sins. No, No! That would not be good for us. He must rather be a Savior and Redeemer from real, great, and grievous, and damnable transgressions and iniquities, yea, from the very greatest and most shocking sins; to be brief, from all sins added together in a grand total.

How many preachers would do that for a fallen brother today? How many reputable men would be willing to bear the rejection of their noble class in order to invite someone who is covered in shame to be their friend? And yet, most of those preachers who would never chance the rejection of their religious group by loving shamed people would consider themselves to be preachers of the gospel. How sad! How tragically sad!

Honestly, they are the ones who are truly shameful! Those who stand in arrogant judgment of their fellow men, those who are tearless in the face of misery, those who care more about honor from men than approval by God, those are the truly shameful!

LET US GO TO HIM!

So, are you a Christian? Whose shame are you most afraid of? The world's or God's? Do you bear His reproach? Do you boast in His cross? Have you come out of hiding to call all men to be healed by the One who touches crosses and makes them beautiful?

One Christmas season I was driving through town and noticed the marquees all around town. They were advertising the most beautiful jewelry people could purchase as gifts for their loved ones. Crosses were advertised everywhere. Crosses! Something that was so hideous Cicero claimed no Roman should even hear the word! The ghastly sight was enough to make the strongest nerves collapse. Yet, all of the stores were selling crosses on necklaces, on rings, on bracelets. But no one was selling guillotines, meth needles, or electric chairs as jewelry. Why? Because they are not beautiful! So why the cross? How did the cross become so beautiful to people all over the world? The cross became beautiful because Jesus touched it! Whatever Jesus touches becomes beautiful. He is the remover of shame. He erased the shame of the cross! If He could erase the shame of the cross, just imagine what His touch could do for you. When He touches the shameful people, He makes them beautiful.

So, dear one, go to Him! Join Him. Don't be ashamed to be all that He was and is. You are His hands. Go touch some of the people who are dying in their shame. Go love someone who has destroyed their family by shameful actions. Go to a religious preacher who is more afraid of his group's rejection than he is of God's disapproval and touch that shameful man. Love him and help him be free to love and serve the shameful King!

Edward T. Walch said what I consider a brilliant thought. As I said at the beginning of this chapter, read it slowly. Here it is: "Our interest in how we treat others is threatening to overtake our concern about how others treat us."

Now that is the way to live life! And, beloved, to live this life is truly an honor! Like Paul, it is to be free from the ones who are truly shameful—those who are too good to love broken and defiled people. Jesus not only joined Himself to fallen humanity, He took their shame upon Himself that He may absolutely erase it and prevent it from ever returning to haunt them again. Follow Him! Accept this honor for Jesus' sake and for His glory.

Other Books By Lee Shipp

THE CRY FOR HIS PRESENCE
Praise Is The Event That God Responds To

ABUSED BY RELIGION, HEALED BY THE CHURCH

SATAN IS COUNTING ON YOU
Resisting The Lure Of Carnal Warfare

HE NEVER TURNED ANYONE AWAY
The Hospitality Of Jesus

EVEN NOW
The Resurrection Of Your Hopes And Dreams

WHY LIVE THIS WAY WHEN YOU DON'T HAVE TO

Made in the USA
Columbia, SC
20 August 2024

40297549R00050